John Young 1662　Joseph Lavington 1675　Robert Mortimer 1680　Thomas Tuke 1682

Joane Andrews　Gregory Baker　Matthew Burman　Thom...　...ne

John Eastwick　Richard Godfrey Ja...　...se

Thomas Gosse　widow Agnes Gosse　Jane Hase　Joane ...

John Least　Jane Norris　widow Jeffries　Edward Mitchell　John Morley

John Hedges　Joseph Oldmixton　Thomas Oviatt　widow Rose　Mr. Charles Shelley

Anne Taylor　Robert Tutton　Edward Sims　Thomas Walmesley　John Young

Joseph Mason 1717　John Bonamy 1719　John Marston 1740　Henry Norman 1745

William Rodway　John Hicks　Thomas Sims　John Shepherd　Edmund Dean　John Keezer

John Smith　Robert Style　Thomas Hooper　Thomas Wilshaw　Robert Rasher　Henry Miles

Edward Lacy　John Batt　William Excestre　John Hooper　Jone Horle　John Huntsley

John Champion　Umphrey Champion　Samuel Tutton　Cornelius Tutton　William Leste...

John Petherham　William Parrish　George Harding　Thomas Payne　Thomas Parrish

John Cavil　Robert Elland　Thomas Porter　William Boley　John Boley　John Fear...

Thomas Mitchell　James Dibble　George Young　Samuel Every　Charles Hucker

William Norman 1780　Bladon Downing 1788　Wadham Pigott 1798　David Williams 1820

Charles Purnell　John Cadbury　Henry Porch　Thomas Greenwood　James Knight

Richard Spencer　James Kington　Thomas Frost　Cyrus Purnell　George Yeo

James Hill　John Ham　William Barnett　Nathaniel Pople　Thomas Jeans

Abraham Jeans　John Palmer　James Staples　Thomas Jones　John Sellick

James Ridout　William Parker　James Tripp　Anthony Hurdaker　John Light

James Every　Joseph Every　Samuel Every　George Dibble　John Amesbury

Isaac Bailey　John Lovel　William Fisher　Charles Disney　Shoyer Williams

Hester Disney　Edmund Whiteing　James Champeney　George Gane　James Durston

James Champion　Charles Handy　David Williams　John Rich　John Prankherd

George Rich　James Rich　Jacob Carpenter　Jonathan Rowland　Edward Spencer

Robert Lawrence 1850　James Trevill 1871　Charles Russell 1886　James Brearley 1898

George Slade　Robert Slade　William Simmons　George Handy　Samuel Pimm

Anthony Badmans　John Weakly　John Cottle　James Purnell　George Rowland

An illustrated History of BLEADON

The CHRONICLE of a SOMERSET VILLAGE

JOHN HICKLEY

First published in the United Kingdom in
2012

Manorly Press
Hillside Farmhouse
Celtic Way   Bleadon
Weston-super-Mare
North Somerset
BS240NF

ISBN 978-0-9574010-0-6

Printed by St Andrew's Press,
St Andrew's Park, Wells,
Somerset, BA5 1TE

I would like
to dedicate this book
to my wife and family
Lorna
Gemma   James
Ellie & Joel

This is a Limited Hardback Edition
of 200 copies, of which this
is number
105

CONTENTS

The end-papers show the names of many of the villagers of Bleadon obtained from documents throughout the centuries

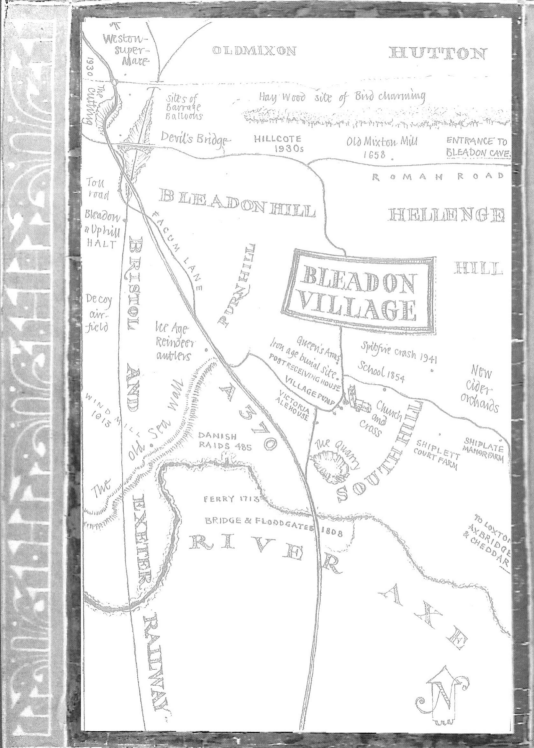

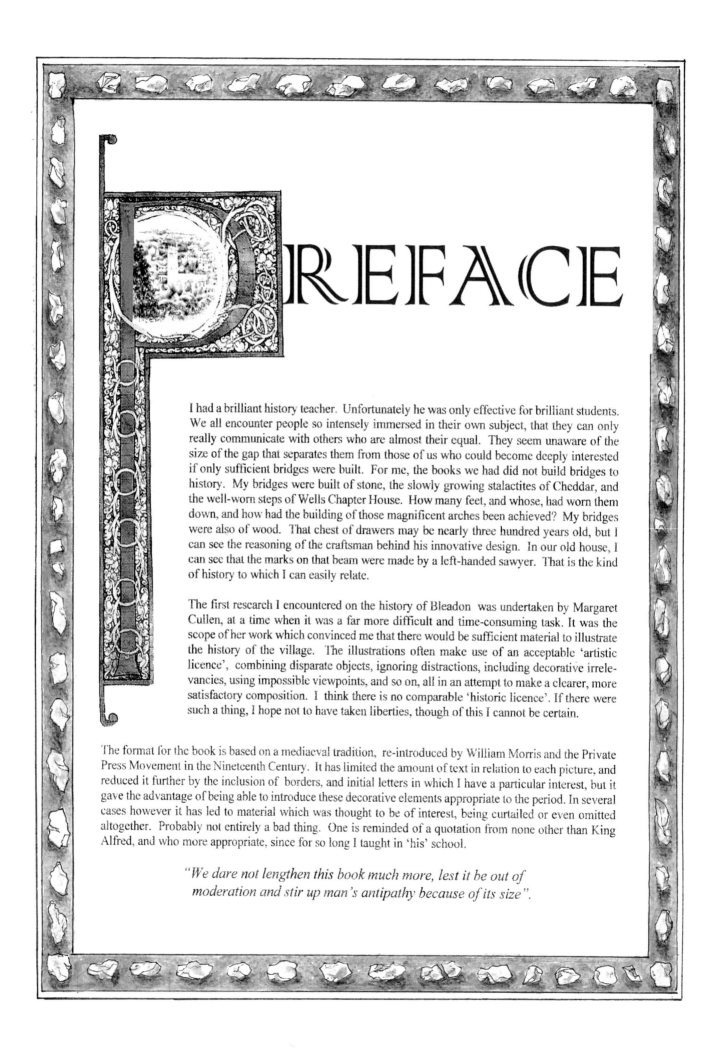

PREFACE

I had a brilliant history teacher. Unfortunately he was only effective for brilliant students. We all encounter people so intensely immersed in their own subject, that they can only really communicate with others who are almost their equal. They seem unaware of the size of the gap that separates them from those of us who could become deeply interested if only sufficient bridges were built. For me, the books we had did not build bridges to history. My bridges were built of stone, the slowly growing stalactites of Cheddar, and the well-worn steps of Wells Chapter House. How many feet, and whose, had worn them down, and how had the building of those magnificent arches been achieved? My bridges were also of wood. That chest of drawers may be nearly three hundred years old, but I can see the reasoning of the craftsman behind his innovative design. In our old house, I can see that the marks on that beam were made by a left-handed sawyer. That is the kind of history to which I can easily relate.

The first research I encountered on the history of Bleadon was undertaken by Margaret Cullen, at a time when it was a far more difficult and time-consuming task. It was the scope of her work which convinced me that there would be sufficient material to illustrate the history of the village. The illustrations often make use of an acceptable 'artistic licence', combining disparate objects, ignoring distractions, including decorative irrelevancies, using impossible viewpoints, and so on, all in an attempt to make a clearer, more satisfactory composition. I think there is no comparable 'historic licence'. If there were such a thing, I hope not to have taken liberties, though of this I cannot be certain.

The format for the book is based on a mediaeval tradition, re-introduced by William Morris and the Private Press Movement in the Nineteenth Century. It has limited the amount of text in relation to each picture, and reduced it further by the inclusion of borders, and initial letters in which I have a particular interest, but it gave the advantage of being able to introduce these decorative elements appropriate to the period. In several cases however it has led to material which was thought to be of interest, being curtailed or even omitted altogether. Probably not entirely a bad thing. One is reminded of a quotation from none other than King Alfred, and who more appropriate, since for so long I taught in 'his' school.

"We dare not lengthen this book much more, lest it be out of moderation and stir up man's antipathy because of its size".

DURING THE LAST GREAT ICE AGE A THIRD OF THE EARTH WAS COVERED IN ICE. IN BRITAIN

it stretched northwards from the Midlands and South Wales. Southern England was frozen, bare Tundra, with only lichen, mosses and a few shrubs. The temperature reached -8 degrees. Water mostly was locked up in ice. Sea levels were low, forming a connection with France. As the land slowly warmed, life began to recover. Animals seeking new food sources came from Europe. Reindeer came, and wolf arctic fox, cave bear, bison, horse, and woolly mammoth. The bones of all these have been found in Bleadon's caves. Reindeer habitually shed antlers in the same place. One of those places is now called Purn Hill. Gravel had been produced by the action of freezing water in rock crevices, swelling and fracturing the stone. Large numbers of antlers were found there in 1899, when the thick layer of gravel was removed for road building. More were found in the late 1920s when the road was widened.

An estimated four thousand people lived in England in the Stone Age. They were nomadic, hunting the creatures that roamed the hills, trapping and spearing reindeer and bison, and harpooning fish. While the men hunted together, women and children dealt with the kill. The large pieces were carried to the caves, cut smaller and cooked.

In harsh dangerous conditions many skills were necessary to maintain life. The all-important flints made axes, knives, spears and harpoons. They were made with great skill and ingenuity, but the nearest source was ninety miles away, on the Wiltshire Downs. Finding the vital flint and collecting it was another skill. It may have been the beginning of crafts and specialist activities. The nomadic life was seasonal, winter survival in caves, with easier hunting conditions in the summer. Care must be taken not to frighten away prey or kill too many. Some must be left for the next year.

One of Bleadon's neighbours, Cheddar man, a complete skeleton of 7150 BC was found in Gough's caves. At the time he died, more ice had melted, the seas had risen and Britain was an island. Forests began to grow, birch and pine first, then more familiar trees. Around 2500 BC the forests began to be cleared and rectangular fields with fertile soil and earth banks were made. By the year 1000 BC permanent farms were established growing wheat and barley, and keeping cattle, sheep and pigs. Man had no longer need to be nomadic. The first people had begun living in Bleadon.

QUITE WHEN IT WAS

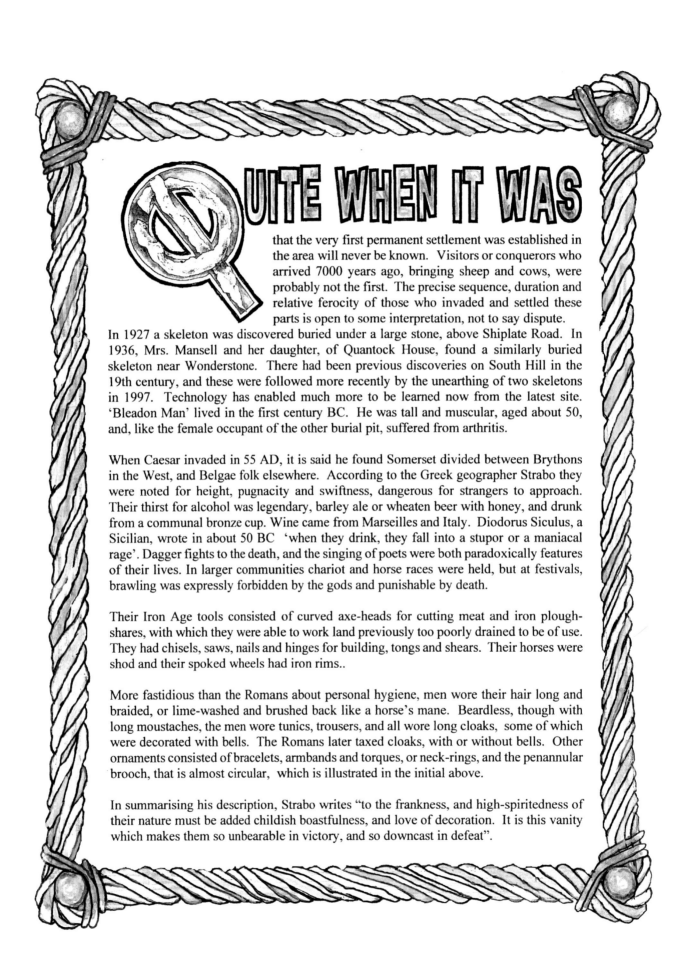

that the very first permanent settlement was established in the area will never be known. Visitors or conquerors who arrived 7000 years ago, bringing sheep and cows, were probably not the first. The precise sequence, duration and relative ferocity of those who invaded and settled these parts is open to some interpretation, not to say dispute.

In 1927 a skeleton was discovered buried under a large stone, above Shiplate Road. In 1936, Mrs. Mansell and her daughter, of Quantock House, found a similarly buried skeleton near Wonderstone. There had been previous discoveries on South Hill in the 19th century, and these were followed more recently by the unearthing of two skeletons in 1997. Technology has enabled much more to be learned now from the latest site. 'Bleadon Man' lived in the first century BC. He was tall and muscular, aged about 50, and, like the female occupant of the other burial pit, suffered from arthritis.

When Caesar invaded in 55 AD, it is said he found Somerset divided between Brythons in the West, and Belgae folk elsewhere. According to the Greek geographer Strabo they were noted for height, pugnacity and swiftness, dangerous for strangers to approach. Their thirst for alcohol was legendary, barley ale or wheaten beer with honey, and drunk from a communal bronze cup. Wine came from Marseilles and Italy. Diodorus Siculus, a Sicilian, wrote in about 50 BC 'when they drink, they fall into a stupor or a maniacal rage'. Dagger fights to the death, and the singing of poets were both paradoxically features of their lives. In larger communities chariot and horse races were held, but at festivals, brawling was expressly forbidden by the gods and punishable by death.

Their Iron Age tools consisted of curved axe-heads for cutting meat and iron plough-shares, with which they were able to work land previously too poorly drained to be of use. They had chisels, saws, nails and hinges for building, tongs and shears. Their horses were shod and their spoked wheels had iron rims..

More fastidious than the Romans about personal hygiene, men wore their hair long and braided, or lime-washed and brushed back like a horse's mane. Beardless, though with long moustaches, the men wore tunics, trousers, and all wore long cloaks, some of which were decorated with bells. The Romans later taxed cloaks, with or without bells. Other ornaments consisted of bracelets, armbands and torques, or neck-rings, and the penannular brooch, that is almost circular, which is illustrated in the initial above.

In summarising his description, Strabo writes "to the frankness, and high-spiritedness of their nature must be added childish boastfulness, and love of decoration. It is this vanity which makes them so unbearable in victory, and so downcast in defeat".

OMANS UNDER CLAUDIUS
INVADED THIS COUNTRY IN 43 AD

At the same time, small British tribes in Somerset joined the tribe of Dobunni and others to the north, forming a kingdom covering six counties. Dio Cassius, a visiting Greek historian, tells us that due to an alliance, they were granted *civitas* status by the Romans, with a capital at Cirencester. Their coinage remained separate from the Romans, until taxes were imposed, and imported goods, like fine pottery became irresistible. Examples of both coins and pottery have been found with other evidence at several sites in Bleadon, on the hill, and in Black Furlong, in Shiplate. The site of a Roman farm was found over the hill at Locking.

Within a few years of the Romans' arrival, a permanent military force was set up to support and protect the mines at Charterhouse. The lead was brought over the Mendips, to the port of Ad Axium. It did not follow "Roman Road", which is not Roman, but which follows the edge of large fields created by the Enclosure Acts in 1760. 'An ancient paved causeway' led up from the centre of Bleadon to an enclosure on the slopes north of the village, 'probably the site of Ad Axium', writes Lieut.-Col. Bramble in 1905. The destination of the lead is not certain. A temple was under construction on Brean Down, completed in 350, and would have used some, but not a great deal. Travelling by sea to Wales was probably less secure than by land, and the shortest voyage to Europe was certainly not round the Cornish coast. Small strips of lead were used as a form of curse, which was written into the soft lead, curled up and thrown into the sea. However malicious the times, this would hardly account for the output of Mendip's mines.

At its peak, four million acres were farmed in Roman times, but the decline of the empire started even before Brean Down's temple was complete. After an inflation crisis in 278, high taxation crushed the bourgeoisie, the rich escaped, but were preoccupied with luxurious comfort, and dinner parties, not the future, or children. Suckling pig, milk-fed snails, and dormice stuffed with pork, nuts, pine kernels and acorns were served under a rose, hung over the dinner table. The flower was a gift to the god of silence, encouraging guests to avoid disclosing secrets. This is the origin of our plaster 'ceiling roses'. The renowned Universities of Gaul all the while were teaching grammar and rhetoric, with little bearing on everyday life.

In 357, Huns crossed the Rhine and pillaged 45 cities, and by 407 Gaul was a 'funeral pyre'. Attila and the Huns struck again in 450, and the Vandals sacked Rome in 455. Despite this, in 460 the noble Sidonius, still in his luxurious villa overlooking the lakes, was reading, swimming, hunting and playing backgammon, unaware of the collapse of the great Roman empire.

By the beginning of the sixth century in Britain, barbarians were camped out in the wrecked remains of Roman villas, cooking on the floors of the principal rooms. Civilisation had declined to such an extent that it would not recover until the days of Dante and Shakespeare.

IN AUGUST

of the year 410, Goths sacked the city of Rome, and their Empire crumbled. The Romans soon left these shores. St. Jerome wrote "The whole world perished in one city." Roman civilization had not exactly provided central heating for all, but what was to come was far worse. Violent raiders in longboats flooded into Celtic Britain, plundering, burning and wrecking what civilization there was; from Northern Germany, Angles and Saxons, from Denmark, Jutes and Danes, and Frisians from Holland. Generically they are usually referred to as Saxons. There were skills and crafts which came with them, but savagery also. In the seventeenth century this became known as the Dark Ages, and with good reason.

Danes had based themselves on Steepholm and from there, plundered either coast at will. An early incident was reported in 'Battels in Somersette foughten in Olden Tymes' It is noted by John Gibbon in 1670 as being recorded on the walls of Lympsham Hall. "The Danes fifth invasion was at Bleydon in 485 where I have inquired of the inhabitants whether they had heard of any Danes that had come in the days of yore to Steep holme near them. Tradition was that a fleet of Danes fled to shelter on said Isle, and sometimes they break out into England, and sometimes into Wales for sustenance."

On one of the raids on Bleadon, stealing food and burning homes, the Danes were pursuing the villagers across the hillside. An old woman, unable to run away, had hidden down by the river, where the raiders had moored their boats. She crept out looking for food, and finding a hatchet, cut the ropes and set their craft adrift on the outgoing tide. The villagers seeing this, realised the Danes had no escape, and rounded on them "with such bloody slaughter as that from thence the place took and ever since hath kept the name Bledon, alias Bleed-down." More commonly and convincingly the name is said to derive from Celtic origins, Blaen dun, end of the range of hills, but this other version does have a more colourful appeal.

This so-called 'Battel of Bleydon, 485' was described in Lympsham Hall in verse:
                    "Ye vessels lay, On Axe's quay,
                    Ye Danes ye swords uplifting,
                    A Bleydon wife, Fetched forth a knife,
                    And sent ye ships a-drifting."

A small victory no doubt against the raiders, but life became no more secure for the villagers when these invaders were followed by the Vikings.

NGLO-SAXON ENGLAND
HAD SUFFERED CONSTANT RAIDS

 from Danes or Vikings for generations. Their strategy was pillage, plunder and then leave. Steepholm was one base from which raiders attacked Bleadon. In 850, this changed. Danes had settled in Kent, seeking to expand their territory. By 867 they were established in York, attacking Mercia and threatening Wessex, the southern third of England. In 871, a series of terrible battles occurred, at Reading, Ashdown and Wilton. Great slaughter was caused. Both Kings, and many chiefs were dead. Alfred became King of Wessex, on the death of his brother. Despite the loss of life, the Danes attacked again,Glastonbury in 873, and Somerton in 877. Finally, Alfred 'with all the people of Somerset and Wiltshire' defeated them at Edington, in 878. The Treaty of Wedmore was signed. Guthrun, the Danish King, 'gave hostages and great oaths' to leave Wessex, and to be baptised with his chiefs. At the baptism ceremony, Alfred was their sponsor.

Having been subject to the fear of attack for so long, the villagers of Bleadon now found their King and the defeated Danes signing a treaty at Wedmore. Whether they were participants in the battles or not, it is more than likely that some would have gone by boat upstream a few miles, and across the fields to see such a sight.

Alfred the Great ruled till 899. His new defences prevented further attacks. He brought scholars to Wessex, revitalising learning and culture. Knowledge of Latin was in danger of being lost, yet many could read English, so he began to translate, "sometimes word by word, sometimes according to the sense." He sought to educate all the children of free men, till they could read English, and write well, and Latin also for those who were to be priests. The 'Alfred Jewel' forms part of the initial letter above.

Tithes had been introduced in 787, involving a tenth of labour or produce, to support the local priest. A Saxon church in Bleadon, like all buildings would initially have been of wood, later becoming a more permanent stone structure. As well as a place of worship, it was a meeting place for the villagers.

By using heavy axes, and massive iron ploughs, drawn by six or eight oxen, the villagers were able to clear forests and settle in the sheltered valleys, whereas earlier people had lived on the hilltops. The oxen could plough over 200 yards, or metres, without a rest, but turning the heavy plough was difficult, so strip farming resulted. Each person had a strip of land a 'furrow-long' in length, together with shared pasture for sheep, but any remaining forest might shelter wolves, which did not become extinct until Tudor times.

BLEADON

had seen boatloads of Wodin-worshipping Germanic tribes sweep aside the Romano-British. They brought savagery and they brought carpenters. They could build longboats but they could also build houses, with chisels saws and augers. 'Sawpits' gave us 'top-dogs and under-dogs'. The latter we naturally support. Their houses had wind-eyes to leeward, which were shuttered. Every settlement had a craftsman who could square logs and joint them, but he worked only for those who could pay.

Densely wooded valleys were cleared and large fields formed, with ploughs and heavy oxen. Strips 200 yards long and ten wide were shared communally between the farmers, as were the tools.

The first document to mention Bleadon by name is an Anglo-Saxon charter of 956, a grant of land of 15 hides to Aethelwold, signed by King Eadwig. A *hide* was variable in acreage but generally considered enough land to support a household. The boundary of the land refers to *cyric staede,* a church farmstead, indicating the presence of an earlier church building at this time.

Another mention in 975 shows Bleadon this time granted to the Monastery at Winchester, signed by Eadwig's brother and successor Eadgar, whose advisor Aethelwold had now become Bishop of Winchester. Eadgar had been crowned in Bath in 973. Bleadon was of course in the diocese of Bath and Wells, and yet given to Winchester. Unusual, but it was not alone in this. The anomaly may be explained by the fact that later in the Domesday Book we see that Bishop Walchalin of Winchester 'held' more than twenty isolated parishes in Taunton, and in Berkshire, Wiltshire and Hampshire, not to mention Piddletrenthide in Dorset.

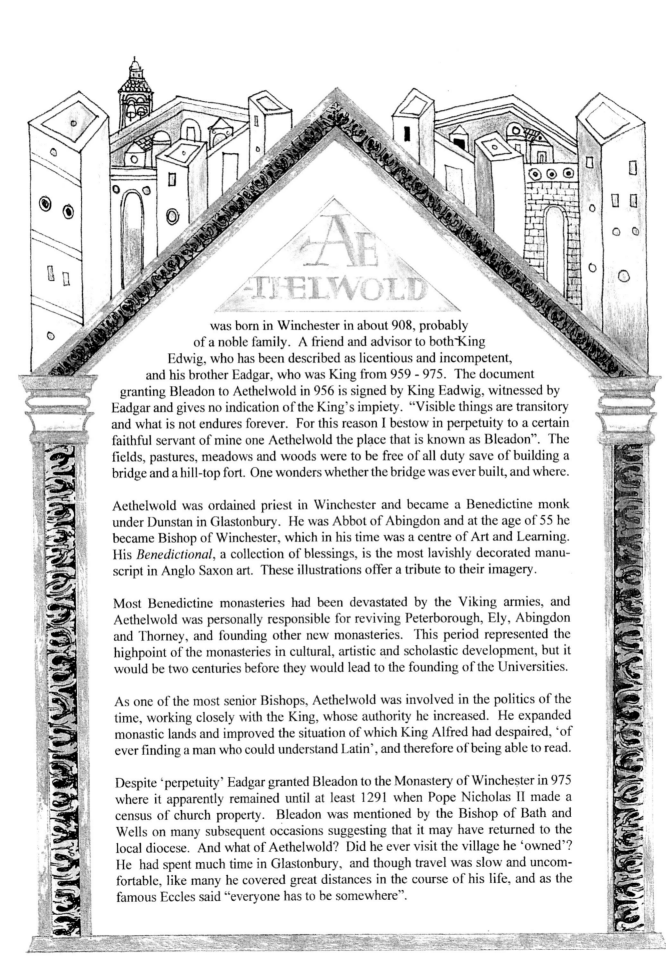

AETHELWOLD was born in Winchester in about 908, probably of a noble family. A friend and advisor to both King Edwig, who has been described as licentious and incompetent, and his brother Eadgar, who was King from 959 - 975. The document granting Bleadon to Aethelwold in 956 is signed by King Eadwig, witnessed by Eadgar and gives no indication of the King's impiety. "Visible things are transitory and what is not endures forever. For this reason I bestow in perpetuity to a certain faithful servant of mine one Aethelwold the place that is known as Bleadon". The fields, pastures, meadows and woods were to be free of all duty save of building a bridge and a hill-top fort. One wonders whether the bridge was ever built, and where.

Aethelwold was ordained priest in Winchester and became a Benedictine monk under Dunstan in Glastonbury. He was Abbot of Abingdon and at the age of 55 he became Bishop of Winchester, which in his time was a centre of Art and Learning. His *Benedictional*, a collection of blessings, is the most lavishly decorated manuscript in Anglo Saxon art. These illustrations offer a tribute to their imagery.

Most Benedictine monasteries had been devastated by the Viking armies, and Aethelwold was personally responsible for reviving Peterborough, Ely, Abingdon and Thorney, and founding other new monasteries. This period represented the highpoint of the monasteries in cultural, artistic and scholastic development, but it would be two centuries before they would lead to the founding of the Universities.

As one of the most senior Bishops, Aethelwold was involved in the politics of the time, working closely with the King, whose authority he increased. He expanded monastic lands and improved the situation of which King Alfred had despaired, 'of ever finding a man who could understand Latin', and therefore of being able to read.

Despite 'perpetuity' Eadgar granted Bleadon to the Monastery of Winchester in 975 where it apparently remained until at least 1291 when Pope Nicholas II made a census of church property. Bleadon was mentioned by the Bishop of Bath and Wells on many subsequent occasions suggesting that it may have returned to the local diocese. And what of Aethelwold? Did he ever visit the village he 'owned'? He had spent much time in Glastonbury, and though travel was slow and uncomfortable, like many he covered great distances in the course of his life, and as the famous Eccles said "everyone has to be somewhere".

LEADON WAS

in the possession of Earl Godwin, the richest man in England. As advisor to King Canute he had been made Earl of Wessex, the southern third of England. It was a powerful unscrupulous family. He and his wife Gytha had ten children, a future Queen, a future King, and three more Earls. The eldest, Sweyn seduced an abbess, fled to Denmark, committed some other crime, fled to England, murdered his cousin, fled to Flanders, and died on his way back from a much-needed pilgrimage to Jerusalem. Earl Godwin had persuaded the King, Edward the Confessor to marry his daughter Edith even though he had killed the King's brother. The marriage was never consummated.

In 1051 the entire family were exiled by Edward, but within a year Godwin had threatened his way back to Earldom. Gytha's exile had taken her to Flatholm 'with the wives of many good folk', and then to St.Omer, Calais.

Earl Godwin died dramatically in 1053. His seal initiates this page. He either had a stroke at a Royal banquet or choked on bread while denying his disloyalty to the King. It may be that he ensured the King's lack of a successor in order to see his son accede, and when the King died, Harold Godwinson did indeed become King, but not for long. It was 1066.

Gytha had given the Manor of Bleadon to the Priory of St. Swithun at Winchester, in 1056. Perhaps she had become familiar with the place during her enforced time on Flatholm, or perhaps during the hunting expeditions to the Bristol Channel enjoyed by Edward and his entourage. She retired to Winchester, a sharp contrast to the little island. Her widowed daughter, Edith was probably already there and another, Gunhilda, a nun, also may have been.

The city was, with Norwich, a rival to London. It had been a centre of the Belgae folk in Roman times, then abandoned, but restored by King Alfred. It had a population of between three and four thousand, and had its own Bishop as early as 662. The Cathedral was started in 1079 by Bishop Walkelin, who owned Bleadon at the time of Domesday. The importance of the city diminished in 1154 when Henry II transferred the exchequer to Westminster. Walkelin's successor as Bishop was Henry of Blois, nephew to Henry I, the richest prelate in England, a great art connoiseur and also owner of the first legal brothel in London.

THE PRIORY OF
ST SWITHVN
WINCHESTER

STEEPHOLM

FLAT HOLM

GY THA

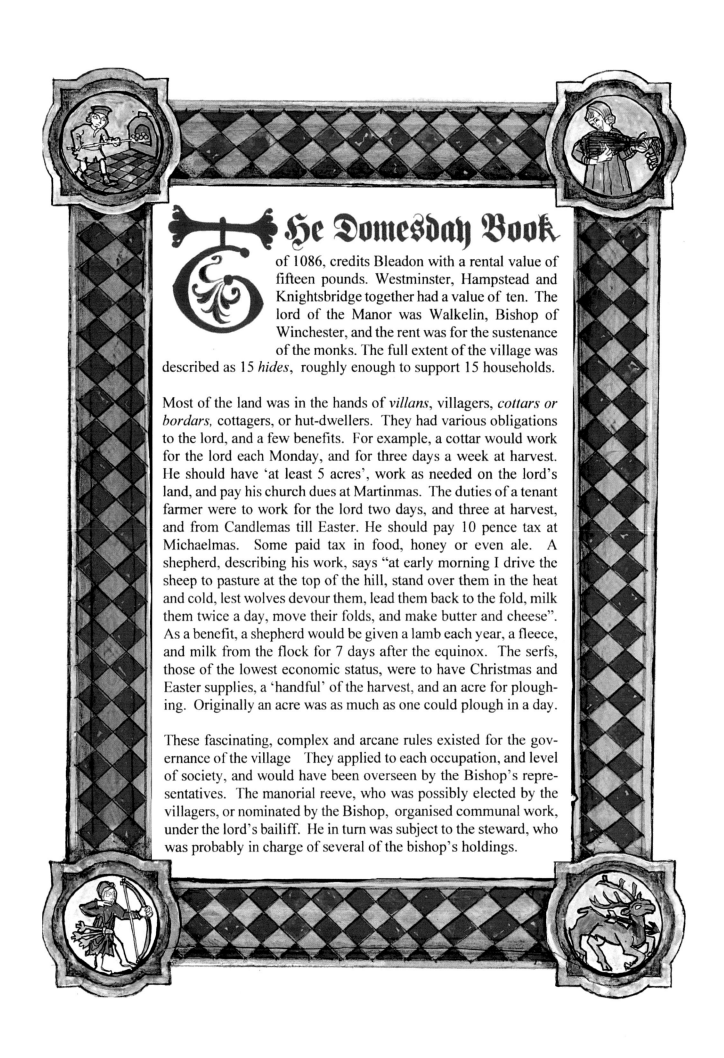

The Domesday Book

of 1086, credits Bleadon with a rental value of fifteen pounds. Westminster, Hampstead and Knightsbridge together had a value of ten. The lord of the Manor was Walkelin, Bishop of Winchester, and the rent was for the sustenance of the monks. The full extent of the village was described as 15 *hides*, roughly enough to support 15 households.

Most of the land was in the hands of *villans*, villagers, *cottars or bordars*, cottagers, or hut-dwellers. They had various obligations to the lord, and a few benefits. For example, a cottar would work for the lord each Monday, and for three days a week at harvest. He should have 'at least 5 acres', work as needed on the lord's land, and pay his church dues at Martinmas. The duties of a tenant farmer were to work for the lord two days, and three at harvest, and from Candlemas till Easter. He should pay 10 pence tax at Michaelmas. Some paid tax in food, honey or even ale. A shepherd, describing his work, says "at early morning I drive the sheep to pasture at the top of the hill, stand over them in the heat and cold, lest wolves devour them, lead them back to the fold, milk them twice a day, move their folds, and make butter and cheese". As a benefit, a shepherd would be given a lamb each year, a fleece, and milk from the flock for 7 days after the equinox. The serfs, those of the lowest economic status, were to have Christmas and Easter supplies, a 'handful' of the harvest, and an acre for plough-ing. Originally an acre was as much as one could plough in a day.

These fascinating, complex and arcane rules existed for the gov-ernance of the village They applied to each occupation, and level of society, and would have been overseen by the Bishop's repre-sentatives. The manorial reeve, who was possibly elected by the villagers, or nominated by the Bishop, organised communal work, under the lord's bailiff. He in turn was subject to the steward, who was probably in charge of several of the bishop's holdings.

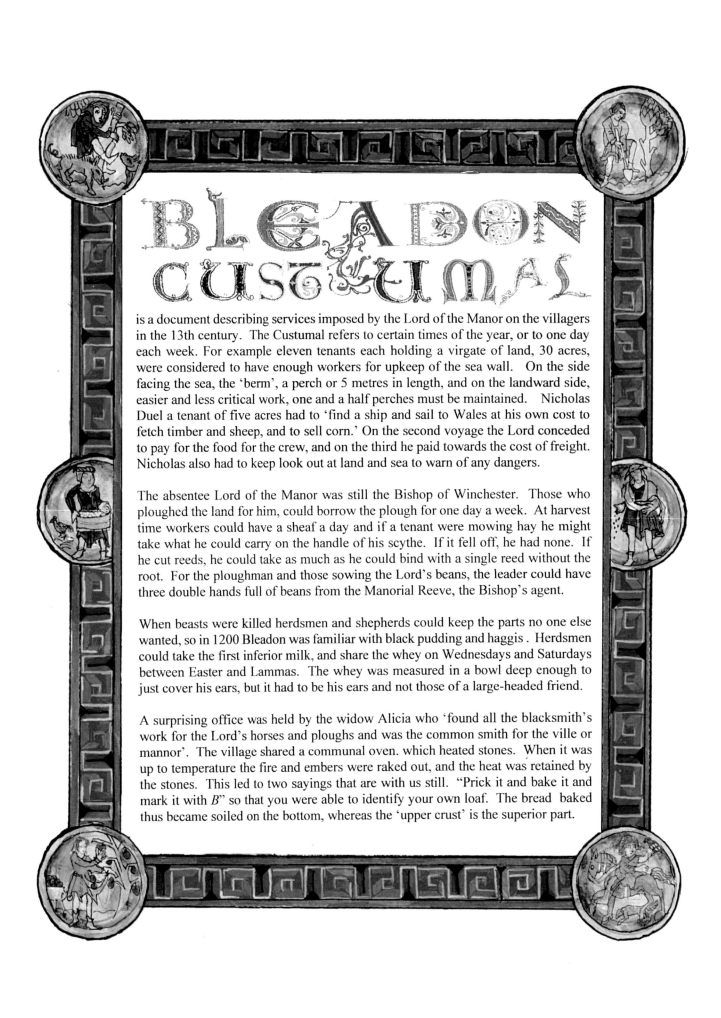

BLEADON CUSTUMAL

is a document describing services imposed by the Lord of the Manor on the villagers in the 13th century. The Custumal refers to certain times of the year, or to one day each week. For example eleven tenants each holding a virgate of land, 30 acres, were considered to have enough workers for upkeep of the sea wall. On the side facing the sea, the 'berm', a perch or 5 metres in length, and on the landward side, easier and less critical work, one and a half perches must be maintained. Nicholas Duel a tenant of five acres had to 'find a ship and sail to Wales at his own cost to fetch timber and sheep, and to sell corn.' On the second voyage the Lord conceded to pay for the food for the crew, and on the third he paid towards the cost of freight. Nicholas also had to keep look out at land and sea to warn of any dangers.

The absentee Lord of the Manor was still the Bishop of Winchester. Those who ploughed the land for him, could borrow the plough for one day a week. At harvest time workers could have a sheaf a day and if a tenant were mowing hay he might take what he could carry on the handle of his scythe. If it fell off, he had none. If he cut reeds, he could take as much as he could bind with a single reed without the root. For the ploughman and those sowing the Lord's beans, the leader could have three double hands full of beans from the Manorial Reeve, the Bishop's agent.

When beasts were killed herdsmen and shepherds could keep the parts no one else wanted, so in 1200 Bleadon was familiar with black pudding and haggis . Herdsmen could take the first inferior milk, and share the whey on Wednesdays and Saturdays between Easter and Lammas. The whey was measured in a bowl deep enough to just cover his ears, but it had to be his ears and not those of a large-headed friend.

A surprising office was held by the widow Alicia who 'found all the blacksmith's work for the Lord's horses and ploughs and was the common smith for the ville or mannor'. The village shared a communal oven. which heated stones. When it was up to temperature the fire and embers were raked out, and the heat was retained by the stones. This led to two sayings that are with us still. "Prick it and bake it and mark it with *B*" so that you were able to identify your own loaf. The bread baked thus became soiled on the bottom, whereas the 'upper crust' is the superior part.

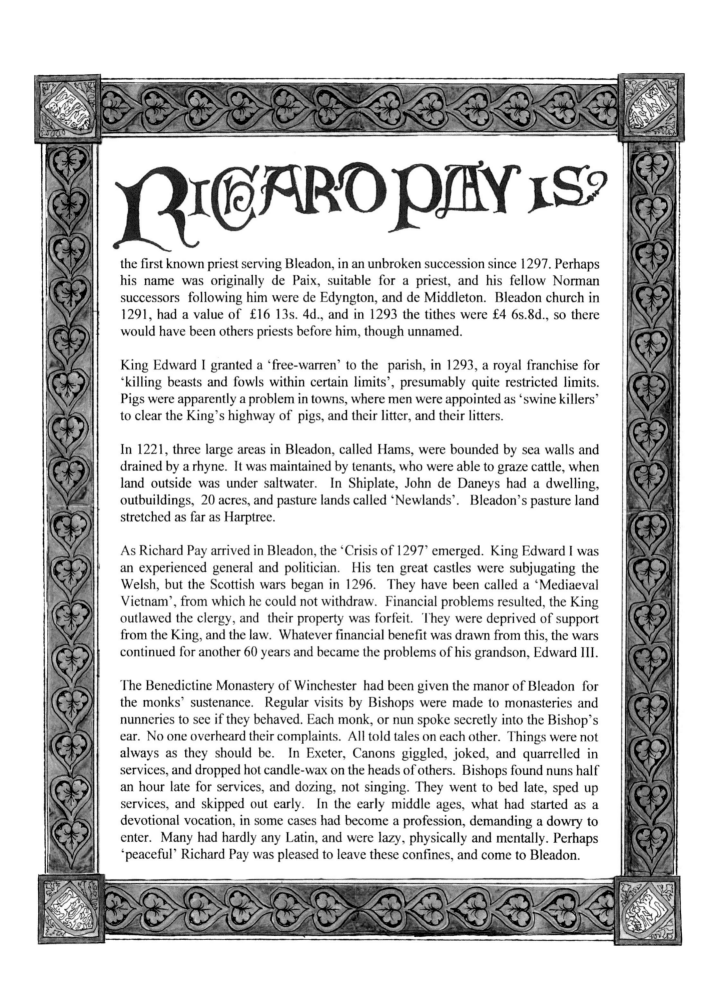

RICHARD PAY IS?

the first known priest serving Bleadon, in an unbroken succession since 1297. Perhaps his name was originally de Paix, suitable for a priest, and his fellow Norman successors following him were de Edyngton, and de Middleton. Bleadon church in 1291, had a value of £16 13s. 4d., and in 1293 the tithes were £4 6s.8d., so there would have been others priests before him, though unnamed.

King Edward I granted a 'free-warren' to the parish, in 1293, a royal franchise for 'killing beasts and fowls within certain limits', presumably quite restricted limits. Pigs were apparently a problem in towns, where men were appointed as 'swine killers' to clear the King's highway of pigs, and their litter, and their litters.

In 1221, three large areas in Bleadon, called Hams, were bounded by sea walls and drained by a rhyne. It was maintained by tenants, who were able to graze cattle, when land outside was under saltwater. In Shiplate, John de Daneys had a dwelling, outbuildings, 20 acres, and pasture lands called 'Newlands'. Bleadon's pasture land stretched as far as Harptree.

As Richard Pay arrived in Bleadon, the 'Crisis of 1297' emerged. King Edward I was an experienced general and politician. His ten great castles were subjugating the Welsh, but the Scottish wars began in 1296. They have been called a 'Mediaeval Vietnam', from which he could not withdraw. Financial problems resulted, the King outlawed the clergy, and their property was forfeit. They were deprived of support from the King, and the law. Whatever financial benefit was drawn from this, the wars continued for another 60 years and became the problems of his grandson, Edward III.

The Benedictine Monastery of Winchester had been given the manor of Bleadon for the monks' sustenance. Regular visits by Bishops were made to monasteries and nunneries to see if they behaved. Each monk, or nun spoke secretly into the Bishop's ear. No one overheard their complaints. All told tales on each other. Things were not always as they should be. In Exeter, Canons giggled, joked, and quarrelled in services, and dropped hot candle-wax on the heads of others. Bishops found nuns half an hour late for services, and dozing, not singing. They went to bed late, sped up services, and skipped out early. In the early middle ages, what had started as a devotional vocation, in some cases had become a profession, demanding a dowry to enter. Many had hardly any Latin, and were lazy, physically and mentally. Perhaps 'peaceful' Richard Pay was pleased to leave these confines, and come to Bleadon.

 AVING BEEN IN BLEADON

For fourteen years and having seen the church building grow from its incomplete state in 1292, Richard Pay was succeeded by Walter de Preston in 1311. His name denoted his priestliness rather than any indication of northern origins. A Benedictine monk, he had been granted the title 'dom' an ecclesiastical dignity. He is mentioned in charters held in the British Museum.

It was during the tenure of his successor, John Astelby in 1314 that much of the building work was completed. The chancel, extending 12 feet further east than now, and the High Altar of stone were dedicated in 1317. The Priory of Winchester was responsible for the chancel, and the village for the nave. A central Norman tower was probably removed at this time, not to be replaced by the west tower until about 1390. The village cross also was erected, but was then within an enlarged churchyard.

In the Tax Roll for Somerset of 1327, Edward III's collectors were John Earle and John of Clevedon. Few people in Bleadon were rich enough to pay taxes. One paid four shillings, one a little more and several paid only one or two shillings. Matilda, Agnes and Christina paid only sixpence. In the following year, 1328, the priest Robert Dalwy having been excommunicated was absolved by submitting to the Bishop of Lincoln, but unfortunately nothing is known of the original crime or misdemeanour.

When the chancel of the church was reduced to its present size in the nineteenth century several original floor-tiles were recovered and set in the North wall of the nave. They date from 1280-1317 and, together with similar ones in Glastonbury and elsewhere, are among the earliest in the country. The designs are encaustic, that is the earthenware body of the tiles are impressed with moulds of various designs, which are then filled with lighter coloured clay or slip, then glazed and fired.

Early tilers were monks, who practised their skills within their area, but itinerant tilers later travelled with their moulds and designs, and stopped to make tiles where they were needed, using local clays and dyes. They sometimes speculatively brought a selection of tiles remaining from a previous project which could be purchased at a reduced price. An idea which has been copied frequently to this day.

atastrophe
struck these shores

in the summer of 1348. Two ships moored at the quayside at Melcombe, Weymouth. One was from Bristol, perhaps bringing wine from Bordeaux, which was then English. On board was a sailor who 'brought with him from Gascony the terrible pestilence', Black Death, a squalid disease that killed within a week. It killed two and a half million people, thirty to fifty per cent of the population. Bubonic plague mutated to the more infectious pneumonic form, spreading from Dorset northwards through Devon and Somerset to England's second city, Bristol. 15 of the 52 Councillors died within weeks and grass grew inches high in Broad Street.

The interdependence of life in villages meant that death rates were often higher. Whole families were wiped out and few escaped unscathed. Two priests in Bleadon, Thomas de Bokenhulle and Thomas Raly, appointed in quick succession that year, may reflect the fact that often 'penitents and confessors were carried together to the grave'. The office of priests made them very vulnerable to the contagion, by visiting the sick or by burying them.

The plague had started in Asia, spread along the trade route, and from Caffa in the Crimea it had been brought by ship to Genoa, thence to Europe. Life in Florence was almost extinguished. The whole of this country was affected within a year. The Scots, taking advantage of the weakened defences, raided Durham in 1349, and took home the disease.

The plague recurred in 1361 and at regular intervals until the end of the century, then less frequently until the Fire of London ended the 1665 outbreak. By then the population had at last reached its original level of four million. Labour had become much more costly, which had a widespread effect everywhere. Cultivation being more difficult, land was put to pasture, which was less labour-intensive, and the wool industry began to thrive, where cereals were needed less. In time the whole of Bleadon Hill was to be known as 'Sheepe Downe', and at a distance was said to represent the snows in winter.

Perhaps the most poignant document of the time is from Brother John Clyn of Kilkenny, who had been recording the tragic events of his village during the plague. Every one of his parishioners had died, and he too was dying. On the final page he writes "I leave parchment for continuing the work in case anyone should still be alive in the future and any son of Adam can escape this pestilence."

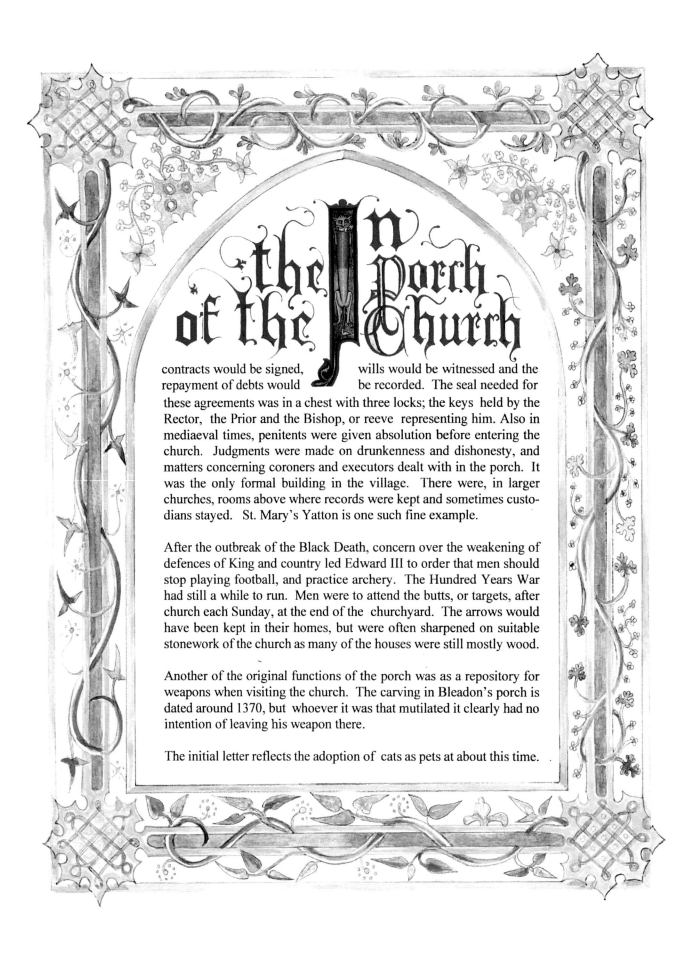

In the Porch of the Church

contracts would be signed, wills would be witnessed and the repayment of debts would be recorded. The seal needed for these agreements was in a chest with three locks; the keys held by the Rector, the Prior and the Bishop, or reeve representing him. Also in mediaeval times, penitents were given absolution before entering the church. Judgments were made on drunkenness and dishonesty, and matters concerning coroners and executors dealt with in the porch. It was the only formal building in the village. There were, in larger churches, rooms above where records were kept and sometimes custodians stayed. St. Mary's Yatton is one such fine example.

After the outbreak of the Black Death, concern over the weakening of defences of King and country led Edward III to order that men should stop playing football, and practice archery. The Hundred Years War had still a while to run. Men were to attend the butts, or targets, after church each Sunday, at the end of the churchyard. The arrows would have been kept in their homes, but were often sharpened on suitable stonework of the church as many of the houses were still mostly wood.

Another of the original functions of the porch was as a repository for weapons when visiting the church. The carving in Bleadon's porch is dated around 1370, but whoever it was that mutilated it clearly had no intention of leaving his weapon there.

The initial letter reflects the adoption of cats as pets at about this time.

Bleadon's pulpit is a rare treasure

There are only about sixty Mediaeval stone pulpits of this form remaining in England, sometimes known as wineglass pulpits, often in oak and occasionally painted. Several others exist nearby, in Banwell, Locking and Hutton, Kewstoke and Worle. It suggests a skilled master mason with his apprentices working in the area around the year 1460.

A wide range and variety of decorative elements is employed in his work to create uniquely individual masterpieces of stone carving. His work in Bleadon church deserves a close look. For example, the lower band of decoration, grapes and vine-leaves, is angled downwards. It is carved as carefully as any part, yet would seldom be seen by anyone. In the restoration of one of Michelangelo's sculptures, when it was removed from the niche where it had stood for four hundred years, features were discovered that were never intended or expected to been seen, and were there only as a sign of the craftsmanship and integrity of the artist. This same integrity is present in the humble journeyman whose beautiful decorative carving graces Bleadon church.

The tower of the church is earlier and dates from about 1390, probably replacing the original central tower, which had been there before the alterations to the chancel in 1317. Church towers are part of the glory of the Somerset countryside, some richly decorated and elaborate like Wrington, Banwell and Winscombe. Although others are more modest and restrained, they too play their part in the scene.

At the time that Bleadon's pulpit was being installed, Gutenberg's printing presses were being carried across the Alps by mule train. On their way to Rome, the printers spent time at a monastery. The monks, familiar with the manufacture of copied books, soon learned the new skills. By the time the presses had been in Rome for ten years, 160,000 books had been printed. Like many new inventions, print mimicked what had gone before, narrow Gothic script. The 'horseless carriage' did the same, until it became familiar as a concept and we were comfortable enough for it to be designed as a 'motor car'. Italian printers redesigned their type, based on their handwriting, familiar to them and us, with its *italic* variant. Despite the printing presses it was some time before William Gyfford or William Wryxham would be preaching in Bleadon with a printed Bible before them. The initial above is based on one from Gutenberg's Bible.

the Law

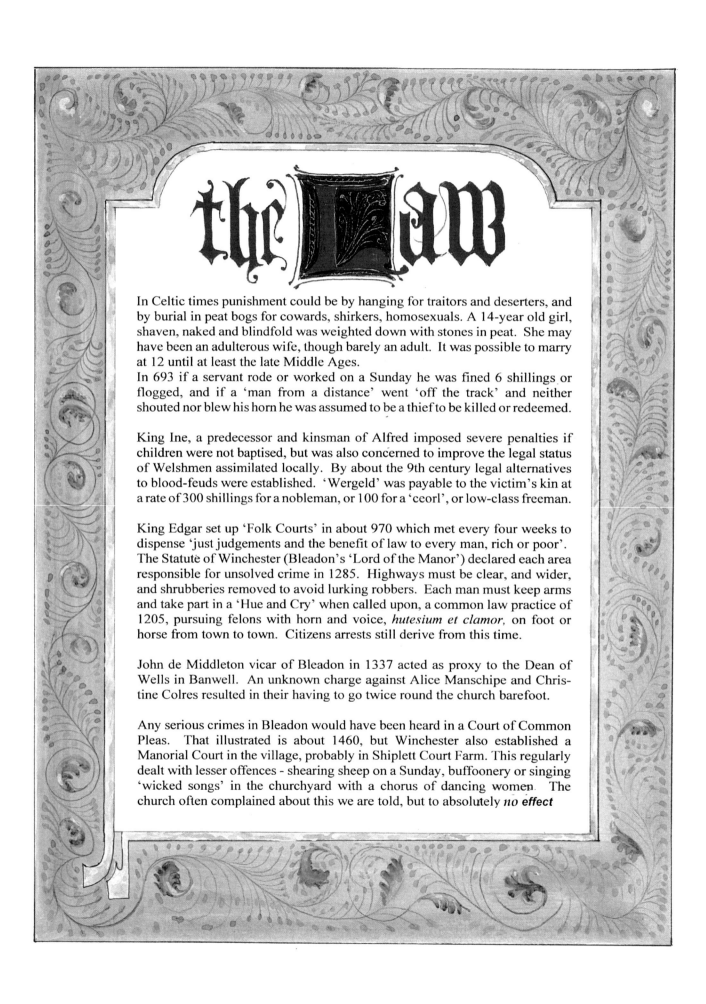

In Celtic times punishment could be by hanging for traitors and deserters, and by burial in peat bogs for cowards, shirkers, homosexuals. A 14-year old girl, shaven, naked and blindfold was weighted down with stones in peat. She may have been an adulterous wife, though barely an adult. It was possible to marry at 12 until at least the late Middle Ages.

In 693 if a servant rode or worked on a Sunday he was fined 6 shillings or flogged, and if a 'man from a distance' went 'off the track' and neither shouted nor blew his horn he was assumed to be a thief to be killed or redeemed.

King Ine, a predecessor and kinsman of Alfred imposed severe penalties if children were not baptised, but was also concerned to improve the legal status of Welshmen assimilated locally. By about the 9th century legal alternatives to blood-feuds were established. 'Wergeld' was payable to the victim's kin at a rate of 300 shillings for a nobleman, or 100 for a 'ceorl', or low-class freeman.

King Edgar set up 'Folk Courts' in about 970 which met every four weeks to dispense 'just judgements and the benefit of law to every man, rich or poor'. The Statute of Winchester (Bleadon's 'Lord of the Manor') declared each area responsible for unsolved crime in 1285. Highways must be clear, and wider, and shrubberies removed to avoid lurking robbers. Each man must keep arms and take part in a 'Hue and Cry' when called upon, a common law practice of 1205, pursuing felons with horn and voice, *hutesium et clamor,* on foot or horse from town to town. Citizens arrests still derive from this time.

John de Middleton vicar of Bleadon in 1337 acted as proxy to the Dean of Wells in Banwell. An unknown charge against Alice Manschipe and Christine Colres resulted in their having to go twice round the church barefoot.

Any serious crimes in Bleadon would have been heard in a Court of Common Pleas. That illustrated is about 1460, but Winchester also established a Manorial Court in the village, probably in Shiplett Court Farm. This regularly dealt with lesser offences - shearing sheep on a Sunday, buffoonery or singing 'wicked songs' in the churchyard with a chorus of dancing women. The church often complained about this we are told, but to absolutely *no effect*

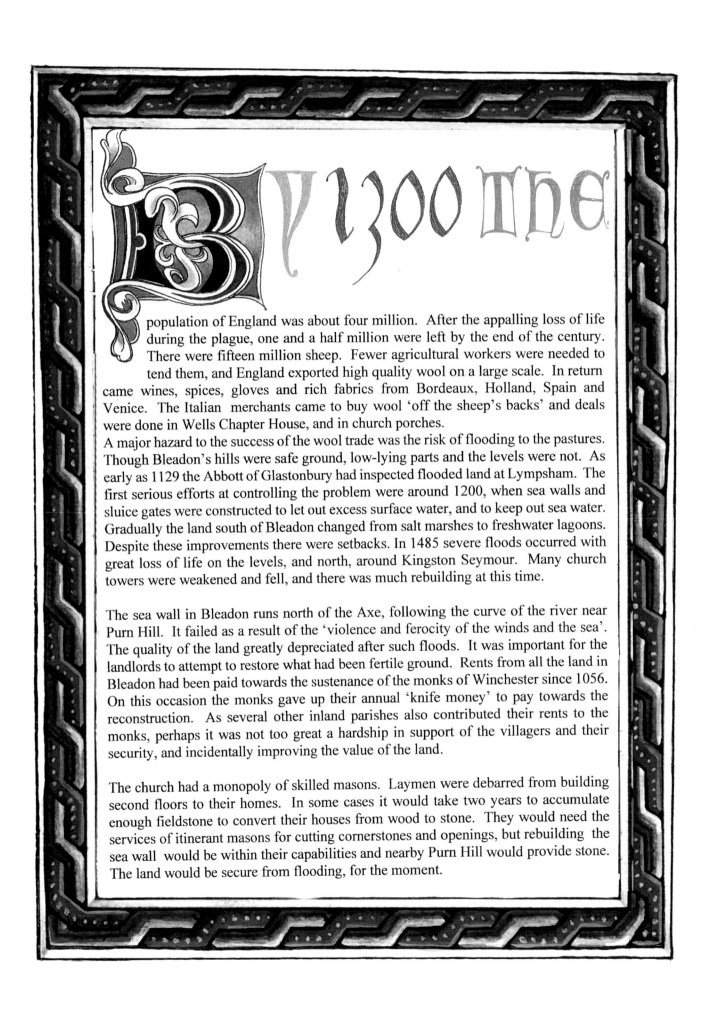

By 1300 The

population of England was about four million. After the appalling loss of life during the plague, one and a half million were left by the end of the century. There were fifteen million sheep. Fewer agricultural workers were needed to tend them, and England exported high quality wool on a large scale. In return came wines, spices, gloves and rich fabrics from Bordeaux, Holland, Spain and Venice. The Italian merchants came to buy wool 'off the sheep's backs' and deals were done in Wells Chapter House, and in church porches.

A major hazard to the success of the wool trade was the risk of flooding to the pastures. Though Bleadon's hills were safe ground, low-lying parts and the levels were not. As early as 1129 the Abbott of Glastonbury had inspected flooded land at Lympsham. The first serious efforts at controlling the problem were around 1200, when sea walls and sluice gates were constructed to let out excess surface water, and to keep out sea water. Gradually the land south of Bleadon changed from salt marshes to freshwater lagoons. Despite these improvements there were setbacks. In 1485 severe floods occurred with great loss of life on the levels, and north, around Kingston Seymour. Many church towers were weakened and fell, and there was much rebuilding at this time.

The sea wall in Bleadon runs north of the Axe, following the curve of the river near Purn Hill. It failed as a result of the 'violence and ferocity of the winds and the sea'. The quality of the land greatly depreciated after such floods. It was important for the landlords to attempt to restore what had been fertile ground. Rents from all the land in Bleadon had been paid towards the sustenance of the monks of Winchester since 1056. On this occasion the monks gave up their annual 'knife money' to pay towards the reconstruction. As several other inland parishes also contributed their rents to the monks, perhaps it was not too great a hardship in support of the villagers and their security, and incidentally improving the value of the land.

The church had a monopoly of skilled masons. Laymen were debarred from building second floors to their homes. In some cases it would take two years to accumulate enough fieldstone to convert their houses from wood to stone. They would need the services of itinerant masons for cutting cornerstones and openings, but rebuilding the sea wall would be within their capabilities and nearby Purn Hill would provide stone. The land would be secure from flooding, for the moment.

SHIPLETT

COURT FARM

FARM HOUSE

HILLSIDE

Living in a very old house provides an opportunity to consider the changes that have been wrought in its lifetime. Physical evidence prompts questions many of which remain unanswerable - when, and why? Countless people, for whom the building has provided a home, lead to questions on what we now call 'lifestyle'. Whatever attempts are made at research, many of these questions too will remain unanswered .

The site around Hillside Farmhouse may have been where Iron Age man built his round wooden huts. An artist's impression of the Bleadon Man site suggests this was so, and it is natural for people to build and settle where others have lived previously, unless there is a good reason not to do so. At the time of Domesday there were about fifteen households in Bleadon, living in wooden buildings. It generally took two years to gather enough field stone to convert them to stone houses, perhaps less here, as stone is more plentiful than elsewhere. By 1658 there were just over thirty households identified in the village.

Hillside Farmhouse was originally single-storied and thatched, with two rooms. Smoke from the fire in the centre of the 'hall' drifted through the thatch. The bedroom was up a ladder above the 'inner' room, amongst the thatch. Later a flagstone floor was carefully fitted in the hall, and another room was added to the east. In the early days the church reserved the right to build above a single storey, but eventually the thatched roof was raised, and a small newel staircase added . A chimney was added in the corner of the hall, supported on two massive stones, Triassic Conglomerate 220 million years old, formed locally when Mendip was a dead desert, surrounded by sea.. The finely-carved fireplace and the ceiling beams were perhaps the work of the same itinerant craftsman who carved similar mouldings in the church ceiling. When the 'Age of Reason', reached Bleadon, bare wood became completely unacceptable, so sitting room beams had to receive a smooth layer of plaster, and the plank doors had an 18th century moulding applied, and were painted a suitable green. When Queen Victoria was widowed in 1861 the acceptable colour for wood became black. Fortunately we now appreciate the natural qualities of wood.

At Shiplett Court Farm other questions arise. The origin of 'Court' has two possibilities. In 1635 John Young the Dean of Winchester leased the property himself. There was a Manorial Court held in the village at regular intervals, and it would seem an obvious choice that it should be held in the Dean's own property. His son John inherited the farm and enlarged it, as did the Yeo family, the next tenants, in 1714. The Act of Enclosure of 1788 removed the Common land on the hill and elsewhere in Bleadon, but Mediaeval tenements were granted parts of the land in compensation, though in return they must maintain the sea wall, in this case quite specifically 3523 feet and eight inches in length. The first of the Yeo family, George, enlarged the farm and was appointed Overseer of the Poor in Bleadon. He was well loved and has a touching epitaph on his tombstone in the chancel of the church. It is possible but unlikely that it was he who attached the name 'Court' to the Farm. His son George inherited the farm, but not the characteristics of his father, and worse was to come when he left the farm to his two daughters, who went to the Court of Chancery over the inheritance. It was none other than the Lord Chancellor who was to pass judgment, and *The Times* had the proverbial field day. The family were no longer the tenants by the time the Dean and Chapter began selling off land in Bleadon in 1867,

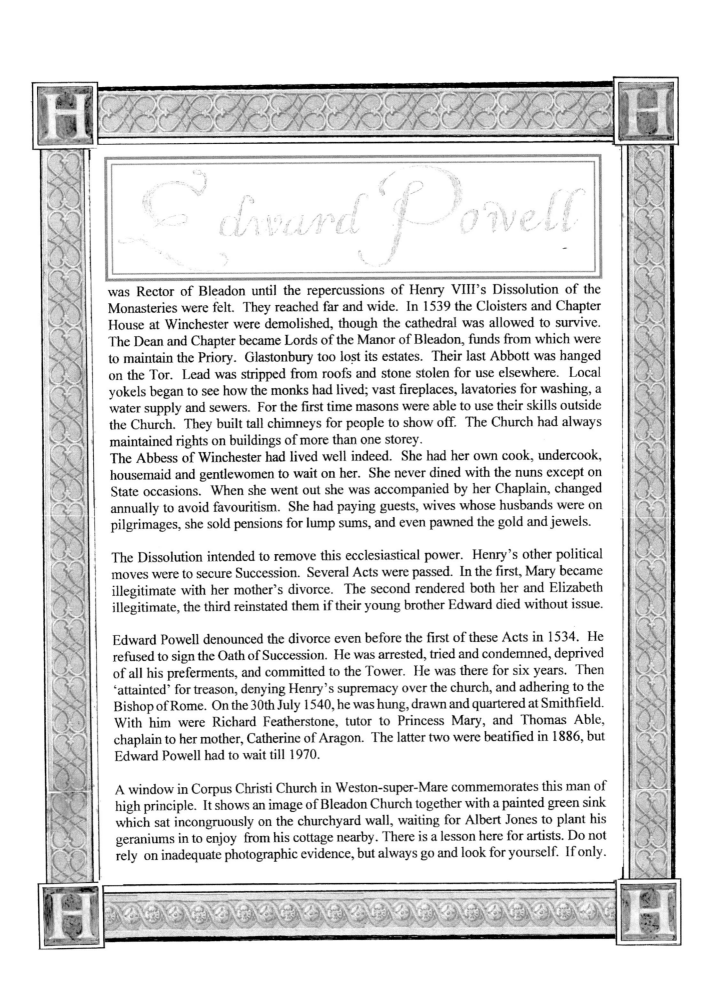

Edward Powell

was Rector of Bleadon until the repercussions of Henry VIII's Dissolution of the Monasteries were felt. They reached far and wide. In 1539 the Cloisters and Chapter House at Winchester were demolished, though the cathedral was allowed to survive. The Dean and Chapter became Lords of the Manor of Bleadon, funds from which were to maintain the Priory. Glastonbury too lost its estates. Their last Abbott was hanged on the Tor. Lead was stripped from roofs and stone stolen for use elsewhere. Local yokels began to see how the monks had lived; vast fireplaces, lavatories for washing, a water supply and sewers. For the first time masons were able to use their skills outside the Church. They built tall chimneys for people to show off. The Church had always maintained rights on buildings of more than one storey.

The Abbess of Winchester had lived well indeed. She had her own cook, undercook, housemaid and gentlewomen to wait on her. She never dined with the nuns except on State occasions. When she went out she was accompanied by her Chaplain, changed annually to avoid favouritism. She had paying guests, wives whose husbands were on pilgrimages, she sold pensions for lump sums, and even pawned the gold and jewels.

The Dissolution intended to remove this ecclesiastical power. Henry's other political moves were to secure Succession. Several Acts were passed. In the first, Mary became illegitimate with her mother's divorce. The second rendered both her and Elizabeth illegitimate, the third reinstated them if their young brother Edward died without issue.

Edward Powell denounced the divorce even before the first of these Acts in 1534. He refused to sign the Oath of Succession. He was arrested, tried and condemned, deprived of all his preferments, and committed to the Tower. He was there for six years. Then 'attainted' for treason, denying Henry's supremacy over the church, and adhering to the Bishop of Rome. On the 30th July 1540, he was hung, drawn and quartered at Smithfield. With him were Richard Featherstone, tutor to Princess Mary, and Thomas Able, chaplain to her mother, Catherine of Aragon. The latter two were beatified in 1886, but Edward Powell had to wait till 1970.

A window in Corpus Christi Church in Weston-super-Mare commemorates this man of high principle. It shows an image of Bleadon Church together with a painted green sink which sat incongruously on the churchyard wall, waiting for Albert Jones to plant his geraniums in to enjoy from his cottage nearby. There is a lesson here for artists. Do not rely on inadequate photographic evidence, but always go and look for yourself. If only.

he Elizabethan Muster of 1569 was ordered to be

held to determine the potential strength of the country's defences. An assessment was made of what every parish should provide, horsemen and footmen. The muster listed all men of military age, their armour and the weapons they held by law, which reflected their social status.

Bleadon's share in the Muster Roll of Ablemen shows no cavalry, either heavy, that is Knights in armour, or light. Very few villages of this size would be expected to have such. Nine Billmen were listed: William Rodway, John Hicks, Thomas Sims, John Shepherd, Edmund Dean, John Keezer, John Smith, Robert Style and Thomas Hooper. There were two Archers, Thomas Wilshaw and Robert Rasher, a Pikeman Henry Miles, and a Gunner, William Rasher. His gun would have been a locally hand-made Arquebus. Firing it would have consisted of installing the supporting stick, aiming, with hand on trigger. The lock then ignited the fuse. Fire! Much smoke ensued. Once it eventually cleared one could see what if anything had been hit. The village in addition had to provide a leather or steel breastplate, three Bills and two swords. To complete the demands of the order Bleadon's "presenters" were then "sworen".

Henry VIII's despoiling of cathedrals and convents was extended by his son, Edward VI. Commissioners who were charged with destruction were nevertheless told to leave "in every Parish Church or Chapple one or two challesses according to the multitude of the people." Some new Communion cups were made from the molten finery. They were of a simple pattern. A bell-shaped bowl on a waisted stem with slightly domed foot. Bleadon's silver chalice conforms to this design and like many in Somerset dates from around 1570. It has been repaired at some time and the decoration may have been added to conceal its repair. One wonders what other form its silver once may have taken.

T NINE ON
THE MORNING OF
TUESDAY JANUARY 20th 1607

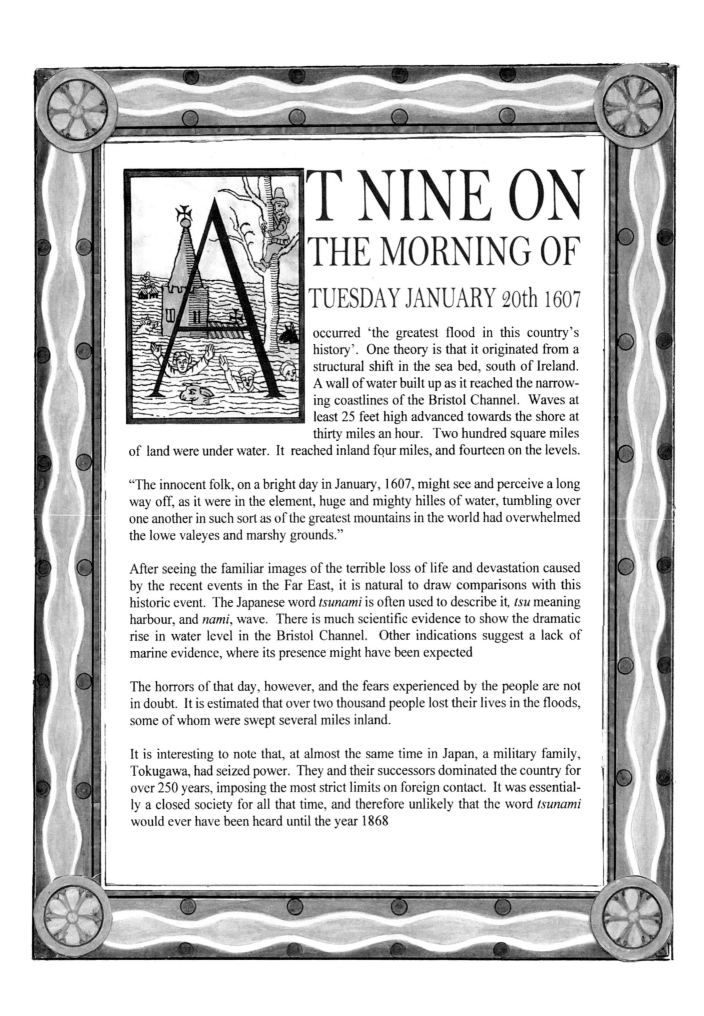

occurred 'the greatest flood in this country's history'. One theory is that it originated from a structural shift in the sea bed, south of Ireland. A wall of water built up as it reached the narrowing coastlines of the Bristol Channel. Waves at least 25 feet high advanced towards the shore at thirty miles an hour. Two hundred square miles of land were under water. It reached inland four miles, and fourteen on the levels.

"The innocent folk, on a bright day in January, 1607, might see and perceive a long way off, as it were in the element, huge and mighty hilles of water, tumbling over one another in such sort as of the greatest mountains in the world had overwhelmed the lowe valeyes and marshy grounds."

After seeing the familiar images of the terrible loss of life and devastation caused by the recent events in the Far East, it is natural to draw comparisons with this historic event. The Japanese word *tsunami* is often used to describe it, *tsu* meaning harbour, and *nami*, wave. There is much scientific evidence to show the dramatic rise in water level in the Bristol Channel. Other indications suggest a lack of marine evidence, where its presence might have been expected

The horrors of that day, however, and the fears experienced by the people are not in doubt. It is estimated that over two thousand people lost their lives in the floods, some of whom were swept several miles inland.

It is interesting to note that, at almost the same time in Japan, a military family, Tokugawa, had seized power. They and their successors dominated the country for over 250 years, imposing the most strict limits on foreign contact. It was essentially a closed society for all that time, and therefore unlikely that the word *tsunami* would ever have been heard until the year 1868

ith all coastal

communities, the residents of Bleadon shared perpetual concern about flooding from the sea. As early as 1500 it was estimated that 70,000 acres in Somerset were liable to flood. In Bleadon, being at the northern edge of the levels, hill grazing on the slopes of the Mendips was traditionally possible on the "Sheepe Downe of the Mannor". In contrast, sheep in Mark for example were lost by the thousand in flood conditions.

Bleadon's Old Sea Wall had been built to protect the area on the northern bank of the tidal River Axe, known as The Western Leases. Many of the villagers worked plots of land of various sizes there, so the effectiveness of the wall and its maintenance were critical in retaining the productivity and value of the land.

The wall, a wide earth bank between trenches, unfortunately proved insufficient against the devastating flood of 1607. Dutch expertise was sought and in 1613, for the first time in this country, two windmills were built to drain the land. One of them was built in Bleadon, near to Purn Hill, the other north of Glastonbury on Common Moor. The King himself, James the First (Sixth), somewhat reminiscent of Canute, said he was "unwilling to allow waterlogged lands to lie waste and unprofitable". His Royal encouragement no doubt spurred on efforts, though later the Crown interests were sold off, in an early form of privatisation, to Sir Cornelius Vermuyden. He it was who had exhibited the expertise, and was to draw up plans to drain the Fens later in 1629, although these met with real problems. In East Anglia new rivers, each twenty miles long drained the land effectively but the dry peat land was subject to shrinkage and ended at a lower level than the rivers that had been built to drain it. Problems with the project in Somerset though were of man's making, due to the onset of the Civil War.

Despite all these efforts, further damaging storms occurred in 1703, when four feet of water again flooded over the sea wall, and in 1799 floods filled the Axe valley with sea water. South of Bleadon, the levels were slowly reclaimed from 1750 onwards by rhynes and sea walls, and the King's Sedgmoor Drain was finished in 1791.

Through all this effort and expense, the value of land and its fertility could be greatly enhanced, when the depth of salinity and risk of flooding was reduced. Land that had been worth as little as 6d. or even 4d. per acre, became productive and worth 3s.4d., 3s.6d. or even 6s.8d. an acre. The fundamental struggle to improve the quality of the land has persisted for centuries. It is only in comparatively very recent times that the danger of serious flooding has come near to being eliminated.

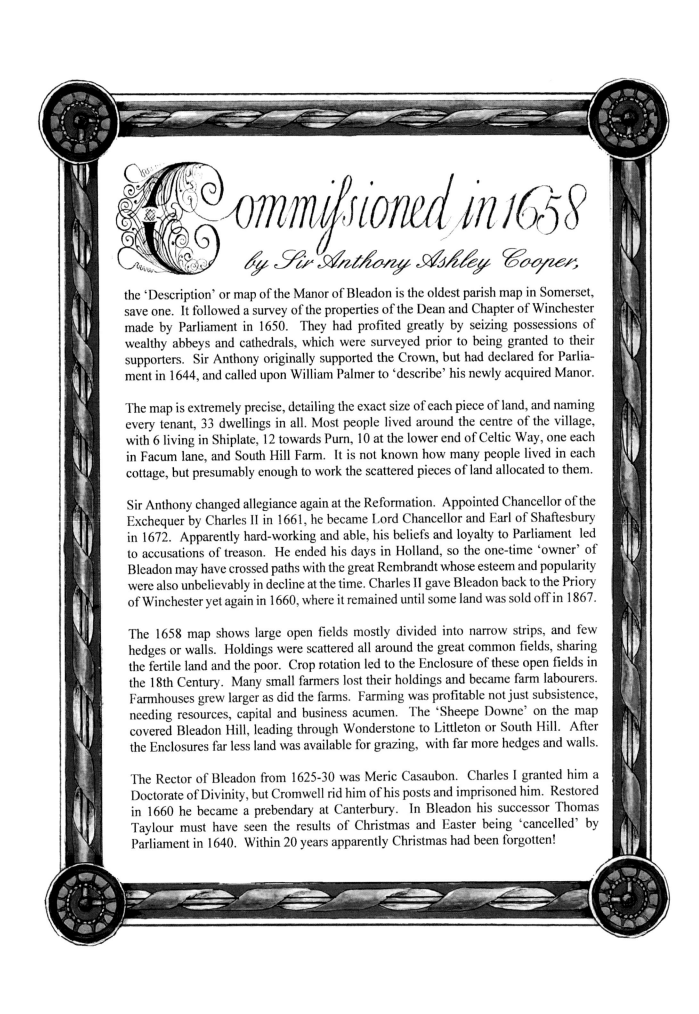

Commissioned in 1658 by Sir Anthony Ashley Cooper,

the 'Description' or map of the Manor of Bleadon is the oldest parish map in Somerset, save one. It followed a survey of the properties of the Dean and Chapter of Winchester made by Parliament in 1650. They had profited greatly by seizing possessions of wealthy abbeys and cathedrals, which were surveyed prior to being granted to their supporters. Sir Anthony originally supported the Crown, but had declared for Parliament in 1644, and called upon William Palmer to 'describe' his newly acquired Manor.

The map is extremely precise, detailing the exact size of each piece of land, and naming every tenant, 33 dwellings in all. Most people lived around the centre of the village, with 6 living in Shiplate, 12 towards Purn, 10 at the lower end of Celtic Way, one each in Facum lane, and South Hill Farm. It is not known how many people lived in each cottage, but presumably enough to work the scattered pieces of land allocated to them.

Sir Anthony changed allegiance again at the Reformation. Appointed Chancellor of the Exchequer by Charles II in 1661, he became Lord Chancellor and Earl of Shaftesbury in 1672. Apparently hard-working and able, his beliefs and loyalty to Parliament led to accusations of treason. He ended his days in Holland, so the one-time 'owner' of Bleadon may have crossed paths with the great Rembrandt whose esteem and popularity were also unbelievably in decline at the time. Charles II gave Bleadon back to the Priory of Winchester yet again in 1660, where it remained until some land was sold off in 1867.

The 1658 map shows large open fields mostly divided into narrow strips, and few hedges or walls. Holdings were scattered all around the great common fields, sharing the fertile land and the poor. Crop rotation led to the Enclosure of these open fields in the 18th Century. Many small farmers lost their holdings and became farm labourers. Farmhouses grew larger as did the farms. Farming was profitable not just subsistence, needing resources, capital and business acumen. The 'Sheepe Downe' on the map covered Bleadon Hill, leading through Wonderstone to Littleton or South Hill. After the Enclosures far less land was available for grazing, with far more hedges and walls.

The Rector of Bleadon from 1625-30 was Meric Casaubon. Charles I granted him a Doctorate of Divinity, but Cromwell rid him of his posts and imprisoned him. Restored in 1660 he became a prebendary at Canterbury. In Bleadon his successor Thomas Taylour must have seen the results of Christmas and Easter being 'cancelled' by Parliament in 1640. Within 20 years apparently Christmas had been forgotten!

HEN THE BELLS WERE INSTALLED IN THE

Tower of the church, they were hung in an unusual anti-clockwise form, shared with those of Bath Abbey. Five of the six bells were cast by Edward Bilbie in 1711.

The Bilbies were an extensive family and prolific in the casting of bells. They were described as wild-looking men with long hair, who could scarcely read or write, and never cast bells except it be at midnight, full moon and perfectly still. So many bells were cast by generations of Bilbies, three Edwards, two Thomases, John, Abraham and William, that it seems unlikely that these demanding conditions were always met. They used several foundries, some quite small, Closworthy, Cullompton and Chew Stoke among them. William and Abraham cast 352 bells in Devon alone. More locally, Bilbie's work appears, and sounds, in Axbridge, Banwell, St. Mary Redcliffe, Chew Stoke, Glastonbury, Uphill old church, Wraxall and Wrington..

Bells are often inscribed. In Bleadon's case the tenor bell reads "When all we were cast, Bilbie cast wee 1711. John Champion Vmphry Champion Churchwardens". Inscriptions elsewhere were sometimes informative - "Bilbie the founder, Bush the hanger, Heathfield's the man that rings the tenor", at Cullompton, or competitive and challenging from a rival - "Bilbie and Boosh may come and see, what Evans and Nott have done by me", at Backwell.

In Bleadon the ringing chamber was forty feet below the belfry with very long draughts on the bellropes. Sam Preston's bill in 1766 for 'laying the bell loft and middle loft was £3 11s. 11d, and James Bayley's for 'cutting and making a way through ye tower into ye middle loft' was 8s.9d. At the same time, lead was replaced on the church tower and evidence found that there had been an earlier central tower.

Part of the frame supporting the bells is dated 1627, earlier than Bilbie's bells were hung, but bells were heard, and heard of far earlier. In Bridgwater, a bell was cast for the church before the end of the thirteenth century by public donation of metal. Leaden vessels, trivets, brass pots and a 'bason with laver' were included. The master founder it is said may not have been resident in the town. A much earlier Bilbie perhaps?

Ferry Crossings

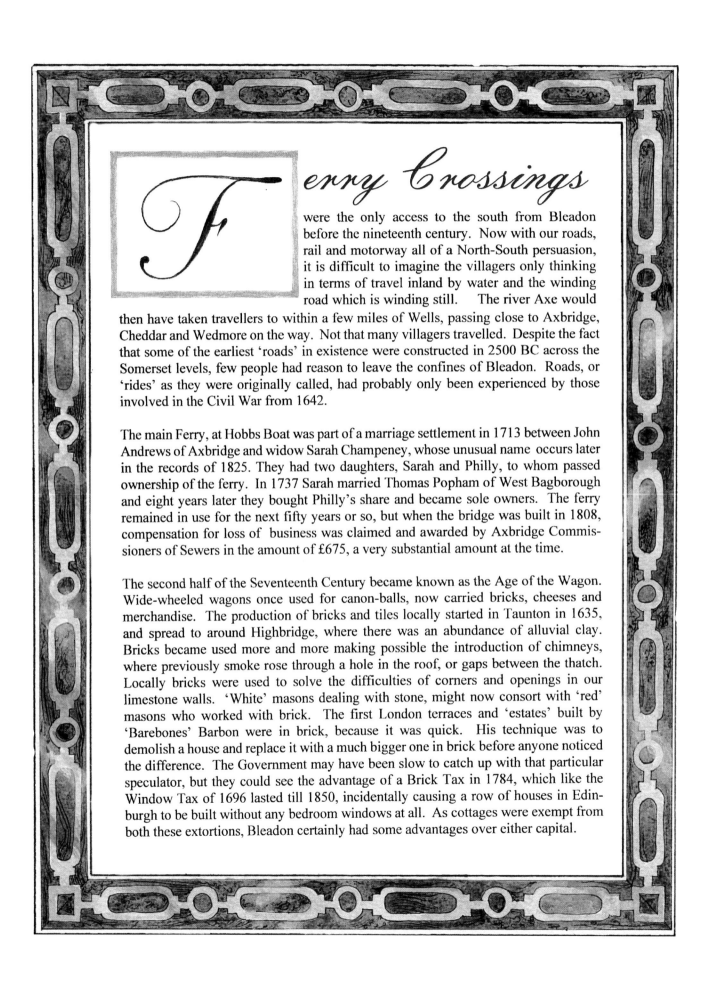

were the only access to the south from Bleadon before the nineteenth century. Now with our roads, rail and motorway all of a North-South persuasion, it is difficult to imagine the villagers only thinking in terms of travel inland by water and the winding road which is winding still. The river Axe would then have taken travellers to within a few miles of Wells, passing close to Axbridge, Cheddar and Wedmore on the way. Not that many villagers travelled. Despite the fact that some of the earliest 'roads' in existence were constructed in 2500 BC across the Somerset levels, few people had reason to leave the confines of Bleadon. Roads, or 'rides' as they were originally called, had probably only been experienced by those involved in the Civil War from 1642.

The main Ferry, at Hobbs Boat was part of a marriage settlement in 1713 between John Andrews of Axbridge and widow Sarah Champeney, whose unusual name occurs later in the records of 1825. They had two daughters, Sarah and Philly, to whom passed ownership of the ferry. In 1737 Sarah married Thomas Popham of West Bagborough and eight years later they bought Philly's share and became sole owners. The ferry remained in use for the next fifty years or so, but when the bridge was built in 1808, compensation for loss of business was claimed and awarded by Axbridge Commissioners of Sewers in the amount of £675, a very substantial amount at the time.

The second half of the Seventeenth Century became known as the Age of the Wagon. Wide-wheeled wagons once used for canon-balls, now carried bricks, cheeses and merchandise. The production of bricks and tiles locally started in Taunton in 1635, and spread to around Highbridge, where there was an abundance of alluvial clay. Bricks became used more and more making possible the introduction of chimneys, where previously smoke rose through a hole in the roof, or gaps between the thatch. Locally bricks were used to solve the difficulties of corners and openings in our limestone walls. 'White' masons dealing with stone, might now consort with 'red' masons who worked with brick. The first London terraces and 'estates' built by 'Barebones' Barbon were in brick, because it was quick. His technique was to demolish a house and replace it with a much bigger one in brick before anyone noticed the difference. The Government may have been slow to catch up with that particular speculator, but they could see the advantage of a Brick Tax in 1784, which like the Window Tax of 1696 lasted till 1850, incidentally causing a row of houses in Edinburgh to be built without any bedroom windows at all. As cottages were exempt from both these extortions, Bleadon certainly had some advantages over either capital.

Rev. William Norman Vicar of Bleadon

took up his post in 1780 on the death of his father Henry who had been vicar for 35 years, and had been regarded as 'a kind-hearted old man who behaved like a good faithful shepherd'. A pupil said "God grant this Parish may have a successor equally serviceable."

William was not the only son to enter the church. His brother, Henry, was Rector of Morestead, near Winchester. However, by 1788 he had become increasingly 'deranged in his intellects' and it was suggested he should visit his brother at the family home for security. His condition led to his parting statement being ignored, that he would "be back as soon as he had killed his brother." Once in Bleadon he showed signs of a more serene state, and care became more relaxed. William was sitting with a friend at supper one evening when he saw Henry take a large knife, and go to the kitchen. A servant was called to take it from him, but he not surprisingly 'omitted to do so'. Henry returned to the parlour unobserved and stabbed his brother twice in the back. "The unfortunate gentleman lay in the greatest agonies for two days before he expired". Rev. Henry Norman was then confined to a private madhouse.

The supper William was enjoying with his friend before being so unkindly interrupted was perhaps Cheddar cheese and a bottle of claret from Bristol, or cold meat and a glass of local ale, and served on the best china, with fine cutlery, on a polished mahogany table. Not only was the table polished, the brass doorknobs and handles were too. There was a great deal of brass to polish in the Eighteenth century. The Bristol Brass Wire company was the 'most considerable brass house in Europe' and the calamine, zinc carbonate, which was combined with copper to make it, came from the Mendips.

In Shiplate, extraction was easy, where it was not embedded in rock. In 1791 a group of Cornish miners acquired a lease for 21 years to extract minerals from Hellenge and Purn Hill with the provision that the land must be completely reinstated after their workings. They left after only three years, so it seems to have been less profitable than they had hoped. A local map of 1791 shows an 'Ochre House' near Hobbs Boat which certainly would have been profitable since all the local whitewashed cottages used it for pigment.

For priests entertaining their friends in earlier centuries things would have been quite different. In the Middle Ages, a slice of bread in place of the plate, or a 'tagliere' or board which would be shared between two diners. Spoons were special and you took your own. Breughel paintings show them tucked in the hat-bands. Earlier still, there were no forks either. They came in the eleventh century. Knives though have always been around and that, combined with a mad brother led to the unhappy end of Rev. William Norman.

LOODGATES
WERE INSTALLED
WHEN BLEADON BRIDGE

was built across the river in 1808. The passing of the Axe Drainage Act of 1802 allowed both this and the digging of the cut which had changed the course of the river. Coal brought from Wales had previously been landed at Shiplate, and coal, brick, timber and salt had been taken as far as Axbridge. There were ferries at Hobbs Boatyard, and at White House Lane, but until then, no road southwards. Nor did the fishing village of Weston, with its smaller population, have any road southwards, even to Uphill.

The engineering of the bridge, an achievement in itself, provided a change in attitude in those who were now able to use it. For the villagers familiar with the sight of vessels slowly passing west and east along the river, there was the new concept of much easier travel from north to south, by foot, by horse, by wagon or carriage. Perhaps the nearest equivalent in our own time is in the way in which we now view the Bristol Channel and its two bridges.

With the building of Bleadon's bridge came increasing association with Lympsham and Brent, now at least as accessible as Cheddar and Axbridge. The road to the south would become more important. McAdam, appointed surveyor-general of roads in the Bristol area, was to develop 3,700 miles of turnpike roads. The road from Bleadon to Uphill was one such.

Large amounts of stone from Bleadon were bought by those in charge of the roads to the south. It was now more easily obtained, and more necessary because of the increase in traffic. Some years later, an official involved with such purchases suffered a tragic loss connected with the bridge. On their way to school in Lympsham, three boys from the families of James Rich and Jacob Carpenter fell from the bridge into the river. The boys were pulled from the river, but one of them did not survive, and it had been his father who had attempted the rescue.

The floodgates were the latest and most powerful attempts yet to solve the perpetual problem of flooding. Highbridge had installed a new bridge and sluice in 1801. It had cost £3450, paid in seven instalments. By comparison, the keeper's salary was just £12 a year.

Rev. John Collinson, vicar of Long Ashton, commented on a survey of 1791, "the whole number of houses in the parish of Bleadon is about fifty, and the inhabitants 300. The little hamlet of Shiplade contains about twenty houses." By 1821, Bleadon had a hundred houses. Of the 106 families, 71 were in agricultural work. This reflected figures for the whole country at this time. Within a generation, the balance was to change, and the majority of workers would be in industry. The population had reached 518 by the year 1821, with an average number of christenings at 8, and burials at 5. Bleadon was slowly growing in size.

# AVID WILLIAMS WAS APPOINTED RECTOR

of Bleadon in 1820. He was a very large man, "like a Farmer". Many clergy in earlier times looked upon their livings as an opportunity to further their studies in areas such as History or Science. The Dean of Manchester for example left his post to look around Europe for crocuses The Rector of Camerton, near Radstock spent ten years visiting Bleadon to study Iron Age barrows. One on Littleton Hill, now South Hill, has disappeared with quarrying. Another four on Bleadon Hill have now been built over. They would have been the burial places of chiefs around the time of Bleadon man.

The Rector of Bleadon however was interested in caves. He was an archaeologist by nature. Together with a Mr. Beard of Banwell, he opened a cavern under Bleadon Hill which had been discovered by miners in 1770 when looking for ochre. There had been five entrances over a wide area. All but one had been sealed. Inside they uncovered an amazing collection of animal bones, some of which are in Axbridge museum. Wild cat, wolf, brown bear, hyena, fox, roe deer, reindeer, arctic fox, Kaffir fox, bison and a creature with tusks six feet long and two feet in diameter. Other investigations were carried out by the Rector's son, Rev. Wadham Piggot Williams in caves which since have been absorbed into the quarry workings on South Hill. The first names of this son would suggest some connection with the landowners of Weston-super-Mare in its early days as an emerging seaside resort.

Though perhaps somewhat remiss in his duties, Rev. David Williams nevertheless wished to maintain the standard of worship in St. Peter & St. Paul's. One Sunday evening a visiting choir from Hutton had been invited. After a little while the Rector could stand it no longer, he stood up and bellowed "Shut up that row! If you cannot sing better than that, don't sing at all!"

The Rectory was at that time Mulberry House, but with ten children, it is understandable that a new house should be built. It is illustrated in the initial. An imposing house with fine grounds, it stood for 150 years where the present Rectory is.

After the financial hardships and scarcities encountered during the Napoleonic Wars, when food production was vital for home consumption, imports and exports again become possible. A branch of the River Axe close to Purn Hill led to Tyle Pill where cutter-rigged sloops could be moored. Coal and commodities would be unloaded and cattle could be exported to Wales and Ireland. A stone causeway led across the flat ground from the hamlet of Weston as Purn was called in those days, and led towards Bleadon church.

Bleadon Waywarden Book 1824

Every parish was responsible for upkeep of the roads within their boundaries until 1894. Supervising this work were 'Waywardens'. Bleadon's Waywarden book, covering 1824 - 1837, has details of payments made and received concerning the 6 miles of roads for which Bleadon was responsible. At that time there were 518 people living in the village. The tools held for this work were 2 iron bars, 4 pickaxes, 2 sledgehammers, 2 shovels, and a wheelbarrow. The book itself cost five shillings.. The entries are made in a variety of hands, some of which are beautifully executed copperplate, while others show a greater degree of effort.

The manual work it documents consisted of "lifting" and breaking stones from the quarries and hauling them to where the roads needed to be made up. For this, workers were paid one shilling a day. For breaking stones they were paid only eight pence, or as little as six pence for every ton. Surveyors verified the condition of the roads, and the accounts were signed by two Justices of the Peace, a serious matter. To such an extent that on one occasion the Parish was summoned at Wells Quarter Sessions in 1848 for failing to repair the road over the hill. To avoid the cost of defence it was agreed to plead guilty and £20 was spent to put right the defect.

What is now known as The Quarry was then called Littleton Hill and much effort was involved in "lowering" it. That was the main source of stone, but quarrying also took place in other areas, Purn, Wonderstone and later Totterdown. The Powder used in quarrying was bought from James Sellick and his son John who lived at Hillside Farmhouse. In 1830, 231 lbs of Powder and Saltpetre were paid for, costing £7 14s. 3d. It was always the most costly payment in the accounts.

Another villager was less affluent. Charles Hucker was one of the quarry workers. He was paid six shillings for six days work in January 1826. In June of that year we read that "Charles Hucker's hovel was removed". After that we know nothing about him for seven years. Was he ill? Probably not, because when eventually he reappears in the Book in 1834 he is immediately "rising and breaking 22 tons of stone" and these enormous physical efforts continue - 38 tons and even as much as 49 tons each month until the book is closed. Closure occurs long before the pages run out, but 1837 details were obliged to be "Entered in a new Book by Order of the Magistrates". No explanation, merely those words written with the most beautiful calligraphic flourishes across the details of the last payments to be made, including one of a pound and a shilling to Charles Hucker, for his month's work.

The Disbursments of John Sellick Surveyor

From Michalmas 1828 to Michalmus 1829.

NE OF THE MOST

DRAMATIC LIGHTNING STRIKES

SUFFERED IN BLEADON, CAUSED DAMAGE

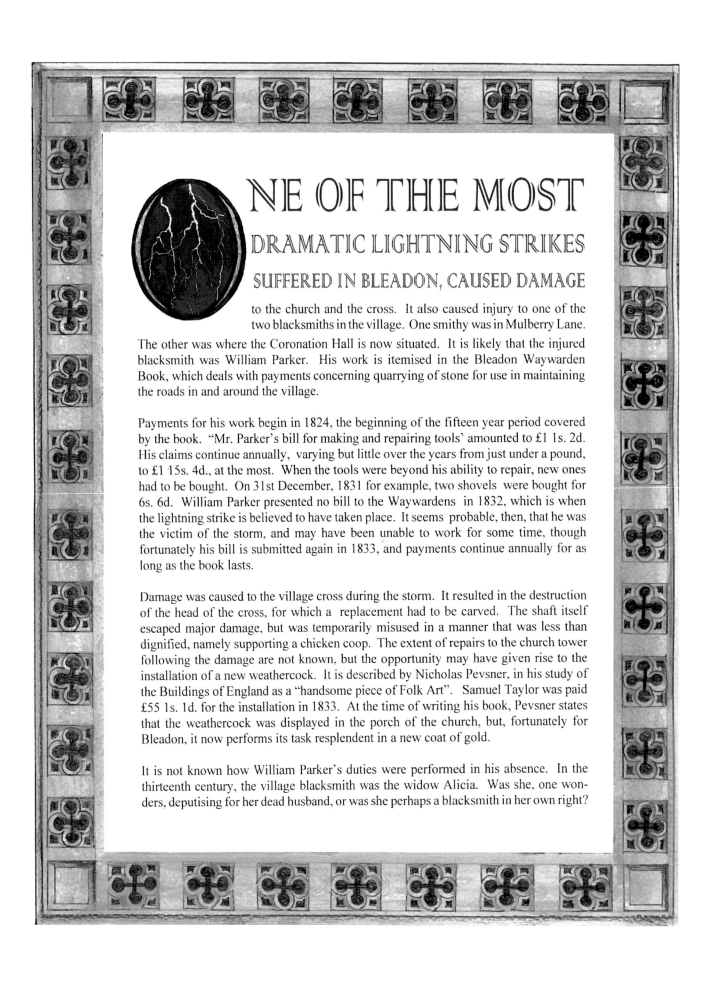

to the church and the cross. It also caused injury to one of the two blacksmiths in the village. One smithy was in Mulberry Lane. The other was where the Coronation Hall is now situated. It is likely that the injured blacksmith was William Parker. His work is itemised in the Bleadon Waywarden Book, which deals with payments concerning quarrying of stone for use in maintaining the roads in and around the village.

Payments for his work begin in 1824, the beginning of the fifteen year period covered by the book. "Mr. Parker's bill for making and repairing tools' amounted to £1 1s. 2d. His claims continue annually, varying but little over the years from just under a pound, to £1 15s. 4d., at the most. When the tools were beyond his ability to repair, new ones had to be bought. On 31st December, 1831 for example, two shovels were bought for 6s. 6d. William Parker presented no bill to the Waywardens in 1832, which is when the lightning strike is believed to have taken place. It seems probable, then, that he was the victim of the storm, and may have been unable to work for some time, though fortunately his bill is submitted again in 1833, and payments continue annually for as long as the book lasts.

Damage was caused to the village cross during the storm. It resulted in the destruction of the head of the cross, for which a replacement had to be carved. The shaft itself escaped major damage, but was temporarily misused in a manner that was less than dignified, namely supporting a chicken coop. The extent of repairs to the church tower following the damage are not known, but the opportunity may have given rise to the installation of a new weathercock. It is described by Nicholas Pevsner, in his study of the Buildings of England as a "handsome piece of Folk Art". Samuel Taylor was paid £55 1s. 1d. for the installation in 1833. At the time of writing his book, Pevsner states that the weathercock was displayed in the porch of the church, but, fortunately for Bleadon, it now performs its task resplendent in a new coat of gold.

It is not known how William Parker's duties were performed in his absence. In the thirteenth century, the village blacksmith was the widow Alicia. Was she, one wonders, deputising for her dead husband, or was she perhaps a blacksmith in her own right?

IMPROBABLE

as it may seem Bleadon had a postal system in 1833, seven years before the introduction of postage stamps. Archives record that an official stamp was issued to a 'Post Receiving House'. At that time post had to be collected and paid for by the recipient.

It was not until 1840 that Rowland Hill introduced the concept of pre-payment with the printing of the famous Penny Black postage stamp, the cost regardless of the distance involved. There was considerable opposition, not least from Members of Parliament who had free post and offered Franks to their friends and colleagues. Hill's postal system depended on reliable cross-country services and an established network of scheduled Mail coaches.

As early as 1635 there had been a method of carrying letters between important towns at a rate of two pence a sheet, for every 80 miles covered. In London a penny post had been started in 1680, which was soon taken over by the Government, and later extended to large towns in the Eighteenth century.

In the 1850's the local 'receiver' in charge of Bleadon Post Office was Joseph Gould. At around the same time part-time postal worker Anthony Trollope's idea of Pillar Boxes was introduced. Bellmen who had signalled the imminence of the last collection, became redundant. The boxes were initially green, but unbelievably people complained of bumping into them. After twenty or thirty years they were all painted red. By the time that was done, someone had complained that 'their' box had turned 'pinky white', rather like one that was outside the Library in Weston. That was repainted in much less than twenty years.

Three significant events occurred coincidentally in about 1840; the start of the Penny Post, the growth of the Railway system, and Victoria and Albert's reintroduction of the family celebration of Christmas. The first Christmas card was printed and posted in 1843. For over 150 years we have bought them, the railways have carried them, and the Post Office have delivered them. The Penny Post lasted until June 1918 when it rose to a penny-halfpenny, but despite its rapid inflationary climb we still thankfully visit Bleadon Post Office to send them.

THE GREAT WESTERN RAILWAY

appointed Isambard Kingdom Brunel as chief engineer in 1833. He was 27 years old. By 1838, it was possible to buy a ticket from Paddington to New York. The railway connected with the *S.S. Great Western*, sailing from Bristol. The voyage took 15 days. Over a period of eight years, the vessel made 60 crossings of the Atlantic. One of several wealthy investors in the Great Western Railway was the Gibbs family of Tyntesfield House, who owned the *S.S.Great Britain*. The recent restoration of this ship, probably gives a good indication of the standard of comfort enjoyed, or endured by passengers of different classes in the *Great Western*.

The Bristol and Exeter Railway was an extension of the G.W.R. At one time in the 1860s there were as many as 366 different railway companies. In continuing the line southwards, two little local difficulties occurred. They must have been as nothing to Brunel, for whom only massive projects seemed to provide sufficient challenges. The first problem was the road over the hill to Bleadon. He designed a single span brick bridge of 110 feet, the highest of its kind, over a cutting 70 feet deep. The second problem was the River Axe. It was navigable as far as Cheddar, with wharves at Rackley, Ellenstream, Axbridge, and several in Bleadon. There was much opposition to the disturbance of the river traffic. One day a fully laden barge with roof tiles sank midstream, blocking the river completely. A local farmer told how his grandfather remembered tiles being recovered, years afterwards. The Railway Board was suspected, but the deed was done, and the river was neither navigable , nor was it a problem any longer to the railway. Bleadon wharf was removed, the Bristol and Exeter Railway built a new wharf at Lympsham, and the line was opened on June 14th, 1841.

The growth of the railway network was a great triumph, supporting the Industrial Revolution. Its influence however was social, as well as economic. The need of the railways to run to a timetable, brought about the adoption of Greenwich Mean Time. Prior to 1852, Bleadon time was twenty minutes behind London time. With the spread of the railways, population grew. At the beginning of the nineteenth century the population of Weston was 138, but by the end, due to the popularity of seaside excursions by rail, it had grown larger than Taunton.

Elsewhere, completely new towns had grown as a result of the railways. Crewe was once a farmhouse. So was Middlesbrough , though within fifty years it had a population of 50,000. In 1838, a little party of gentlemen was enjoying an alfresco lunch in a field. Brunel was among them. The picnic site is now Swindon.

Formal  *ducation*

in Bleadon *began with*

the opening of the Public Elementary School in 1854, at the top of School Lane. It was enlarged in 1874 to take 90 pupils. Mr. Watson was the first Headmaster. Children were divided into three classes. In the 1930s Mrs. Bennett, wife of a farmer in Shiplate, was the teacher for the beginners. Her room had small tables for the children, a round black stove, and a desk and blackboard for the teacher. The day began with the register being called, and news being shared of babies born or family illness. The alphabet was then copied from the blackboard, with pencils into copybooks. Messy purple indelible pencils were pupils' favourites. Earlier times would have seen children with slates and styluses scratching their surfaces, with a damp cloth to clean them. Once the alphabet was mastered, came names, short words and numbers. 'Times tables' were learnt and recited in unison. Bible studies, and nature study were also on the time-table.

In the next class Mrs Cam Parker, wife of the blacksmith, taught in the 'big room'. Desks with lids and inkwells initially created more mess than the pink blotting paper could deal with. Spelling, punctuation, multiplication and division, history and geography followed, with the study of plants and animals playing an important part in the curriculum as one would expect in a village such as Bleadon.

In the top class, the Headmistress, Mrs. Bell taught grammar, 'big' numbers, fractions and decimals, more history and geography. Tests and exams eventually led to the 'eleven plus', with some children going to Weston Grammar, boys, or girls, and others to St. John's school, where Weston College now stands tall. Bleadon School finally closed its classrooms in 1964, possibly because, unlike Uphill, it could not be enlarged through lack of adjacent space.

Across the road from the school, Mr Over who lived at The Mount and Mr Clogg, used to welcome visits from the children who loved working in the fields, orchards and greenhouse, eating much of the fruit they picked. Often they were lined up in School Lane and given fruit or vegetables to take home. At Christmas time they were given oranges by Mr.Ruck, who lived at Wonderstone and who was the owner of a plantation.

It is a sadness to the village that it has lost its school, not least because of the lack of common experience among its youngsters, or the joyful sounds of ninety children being freed each day, but also the tyranny of the twice-daily school run.

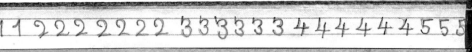
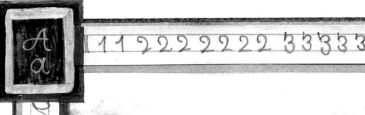

ILLAGE UMPS

were not the only source of water in Bleadon.   Several other wells existed, the sites of which were very important in determining where houses were built originally.

The familiar cast iron pumps are Victorian, the lower one to be used for small vessels carried by hand, and the one above for wagons carrying large quantities. For most villagers there was a need to visit the pumps daily to collect the water supply for the household. While waiting turn, or lingering afterwards, there was naturally an opportunity for meeting friends and neighbours, for gossiping, and for assignations, accidental or otherwise. For many maids, servants or workers it may have been the only chance to leave their place of work during the day.

Those responsible for the supply of water were the Axbridge Guardians, who were the Sanitary Authority in charge of drains for the area. Earlier pumps may well have been much simpler affairs. Elm, which used to be the prevalent hardwood, was used to a surprising extent in water engineering. Whole trunks were bored out and driven together to make pipes for the main supply, and earlier village pumps were constructed of elm including the moving parts, even down to the valves. Considering the 'rogue' quality of elm compared to other hardwoods, it says much for the craftsmanship, ingenuity and determination to use the local material that lay to hand.

At about the time the present pumps were installed, there were 20 farmers in Bleadon, three shopkeepers, a tailor, a wheelwright, Post Office, two blacksmiths a butcher and two pubs. As a more adventurous alternative to the pubs, the young men of the village sometimes assembled in small groups and went 'Charming the Birds out of the Trees'.

A dark night was essential to success. The operators were three or four in a company, and several companies might be at work in the same wood. They entered the coppice where birds were roosting. Bearing lanterns and Charming Bells, they kept up an incessant ringing of the bells. The birds were mainly thrushes, blackbirds, fieldfares, redwings, locally called 'windles', and starlings.   Smaller birds were disregarded. Terrified by the noise, and dazed by the lights they could be taken by hand, or if roosting higher in the trees, knocked off by poles which the lads carried. This 'charming' differed from either 'Bird-batting' or 'Bat-fowling' in that no nets were used. By the sound of it those activities were even more brutal.   Stricter game preservation laws fortunately ended this practice in around 1860. There is a set of three Charming Bells from Bleadon, donated to Weston Museum long ago, which will be housed in the Museum at Taunton.

BLEADON & UPHILL HALT
FIRST OPENED IN 1871

It is due to the Lord of the Manor of Uphill at the time, Charles Payne, or 'Devil Payne' as he was called on account of his violent temper. He owned the land and insisted that if the railway cut through it, a station should be built. It was duly built, but no agreement had been made that the trains should actually stop there, so at the grand inauguration of the Halt, the train did not halt, causing a misnomer, disappointment, and probably even more of a temper. To reach the station, villagers from Bleadon, would follow the road round Purn Hill, and down Facum Lane to catch the train to Weston, a six minute journey, and later walk back home again. If they were going further and had luggage, a pony and trap would take them. Mr. Gilman was probably the last station master, and went to work on his bike.

Compensation was often sought for the intrusion of railways. A clergyman complained that his daughter's bedroom window was subject to the "unhallowed gaze of navigators". The family would have to "recuperate at a spa, and then seek to move". He received compensation, but did neither. The Duke of Bedford, on the other hand, received £150,000 compensation, but returned it all, finding that the railway had benefited the estate. A writer in *John Bull* magazine in 1835, wrote "the noise and stench of locomotives may disturb the quietude of the peasant, the farmer and the gentleman". John Ruskin disliked rail travel, feeling that he had become a 'living parcel'. The Prime Minister, Gladstone, was very different. Not only was he frequently seen on public omnibuses, but he forced railway companies in the 1840s to run cheap Third Class trains for workmen, and would use them himself.

By 1845, nearly 13 million people had travelled on trains, nearly half the population. The number would increase as local stations proliferated. There were at one time eight stations between Weston and Taunton, the first of which was Bleadon and Uphill. In November 1959 it became 'unstaffed' and closed altogether in 1964. Other than 'Devil's bridge', it is not known what part, if any, Brunel played in the design of the little station. He certainly designed elements of the station at Cheddar, on what was the 'Strawberry Line', and there is a familiar *house style* in many of the features, like the perforated valance and elegant decorative barge boards.
At its opening in 1871, the carriages had no corridors, no dining cars, and no lavatories. On journeys to London, though, the trains of the Great Western Railway always stopped for ten minutes at Swindon, for the convenience of the passengers, who were able to buy food, at such prices that it became known as 'Swindle'em'.

THE CLOCK ON THE
CHURCH TOWER WAS INSTALLED

as a result of public subscription in 1897. It represented Bleadon's commemoration of the Diamond Jubilee of Queen Victoria. The cost of Mr. W.E.Perrett's 'lovely little mechanism' was £200.

The Queen had celebrated on 22nd June, by riding in procession to St. Paul's with 50,000 troops, from around the Empire. With the Prince of Wales on one side of her, and the Kaiser on the other, she stayed in her carriage while a *Te deum* was sung, then continued processing, to cries from the crowd of "Go it, old girl!". It was the first time the 'Widow of Windsor' had not worn black. She wore dark grey. Later, she rode around the crowded gardens of Buckingham Palace in a smaller carriage, and sat in a flower-filled tent, eating toast, buttered by an Indian servant. She complained of the procession to one of her guests, the Bishop of Winchester, who had been on the steps of St. Paul's, "I had a very bad place," she said "and saw nothing". This must have been one of the first Bishops of Winchester not to have 'owned' Bleadon.

The new clock would have been ticking for about two years, when the organ was installed in church. It replaced a harmonium, which had been in use since 1855. It is not known who was the first organist, but later a Mr. Shellabear, typifying the longevity of many organists, celebrating 20 years in the post received a gift of £14, and with it was told 'to buy something useful'. Public subscription was again required in 1963, when the clock needed restoration, and unfortunately, at the time of writing, the little mechanism is in need of attention again. The clock in Wells Cathedral, a very complicated and large mechanism is a source of wonder to many. That was installed in 1390.

1897 marked not only the Diamond Jubilee, but also the 600th anniversary of the appointment of the first known priest in the village, Richard Pay. The event does not seem to have been celebrated at the time. However, in 1997, there were many and varied celebrations in the community, under the auspices of 'Bleadon 700'. The Bishop of Bath and Wells celebrated Eucharist, and the Bishop of Clifton preached at Evensong. A dramatic presentation was performed in the church, 'The Cure of Souls'. It told the history of the priesthood in the village, through the stories of the various incumbents, portrayed by local thespians. Other events all helped to celebrate; bell-ringing and folk dancing, flower festivals and organ recitals, talks, walks and sports. Four banners hanging in the church illustrate events from four of the seven centuries of village life.

EARLY POSTCARDS

were not pictorial. When they were introduced in 1870 they had a printed halfpenny stamp but were otherwise blank. By that time statutory Bank Holidays were established, and half-day working on Saturdays. Railways provided a chance for many people to visit the countryside or seaside for the first time. As a reminder of their day out they might buy a photograph from amongst the vast selection provided by Francis Frith, or local photographers like Fred Viner of the Boulevard in Weston. However it was not until 1894 that the Post Office permitted pictorial cards., and only in 1902 was the reverse divided for a message and the address. Perhaps slow to see the potential of this means of communication, the postal service was nevertheless extremely efficient as can be seen by messages on these early cards. Delivery the same day was a standard expectation.

Visitors to the village, like Winnie and the 'club girls' in 1914, could visit Godden's Tea Rooms, on the corner of Mulberry Lane, buy a card showing Mulberry House, opposite, where they were staying, write the message home to Bristol, post it round the corner at the Post Office and it would be delivered in the evening post.

The earliest cards were sepia coloured, but coloured cards were available surprisingly soon. One of a series of Bleadon, which has a stamp franked in 1906, shows the church tower covered with ivy as high as the clock. Another, shown above, has Shiplate Hill Farm on the edge of the quarry on South Hill. There are probably more than forty early postcards of the village, perhaps more. The highpoint of their popularity was within the first fifty years, but by mid-century expectations were changing. The growth of personal photography, even home movies of the holidays, saw the decline of their usefulness. Mass-production had made them commonplace, and now technological development makes the sending of the image instantaneous.

As the sending of cards declined, collecting them began. New cards are not quite redundant however. On holiday, it is never quite possible to take the perfect shot, the ideal viewpoint, lighting, weather conditions, a clear view, and no crowds. So the original local photographer, who started this search for an idealised memento of our visit, still has the advantage. He can choose his day and take his time, like his forerunner, whose early sepia images are now being revived, providing an alternative to the stylish work of the Art Photographer. They are the source material for a local calendar of Bleadon, and countless books on local history. Most of all they give us an opportunity to study and value the fascinating history of our own surroundings.

Miss E. Alderman, Langford, Nr. Bristol

Dear Evelyn, I am sending this from the Bazaar to-day

Love from Winnie.

have you learn on the bycicle yet.

at the concert last night it was Packed

VILLAGE OUTINGS

before 1900 would have been relatively small affairs. For most people excursions started with the Exhibition of 1851. Six million people visited it by railway from the large towns or cities, but from Bleadon such a journey would have been long and complicated. Though the railways replaced much horse-drawn transport, paradoxically with seaside excursions it encouraged such local tours for visitors. When Bank Holidays were introduced in 1871, numbers grew. Wagonettes with four horses or two-horse carriages took them to outlying villages like Cheddar, via Bleadon, no doubt stopping at the Tea Gardens or the Queen's to 'rest the horses'. A rail trip into Weston involved a walk along Facum Lane to the station.

After the first World War motor transport had developed enough to cater for recognisable village outings. The early vehicles consisted of a chassis and separate bodies, so that summer charabancs used for day trips, would be transformed in winter into goods lorries. Charabancs survived only a few years. They were open and could be unstable. A canvas roof stowed at the back, was erected by healthy and honourable volunteers. Wookey still has a sign declaring the way is 'unsuitable for charabancs'. Motor Coaches soon replaced them, the first of which was scheduled between Bristol and London on 11 February 1925, appropriately enough as the very first Mail Coach was run on the same route. Coach visits to the 'Rock of Ages', Burrington Combe, took thousands from local towns and villages.

.

Burnell's Coaches, and later regular bus routes run by Bristol Tramways went to Burnham, Brean, Bridgwater and Glastonbury. Fares were 6d for adults and 3d. for children. The opportunities for village outings broadened in the 1930s. P. & A. Campbell's *White Funnel* fleet with its 11 ships offered paddle steamer trips to Cardiff, Barry, Lynmouth and Ilfracombe. Weston Airport opened in 1936 providing pleasure trips for the high-flyers, though for the more adventurous, flights had been available since 1919 in an Avro biplane from a nearby field. Travellers in all of the above possibly benefitted from *Mothersill's Remedy* for Sea Train and Air sickness, as advertised in the local guide for 1935.

Village outings now benefit from comfortable and convenient coach travel, one provider of which is believed to have developed from local donkey carts. Bleadon villagers now travel far and wide for reasons both cultural and horticultural, for interest, study, diversion, curiosity and entertainment. Visits to museums, Garden centres, Cathedrals, Docks and Grand houses together with many other venues have strengthened friendships and deepened the feeling of community. It truly broadens the experience, though it is good to get back to the village, especially if there was a need for *Mothersill's Remedy!*

SHOPS & GARAGES

In 1724 Daniel Defoe visited these parts and described trade in his *"Tour through the Whole Island of Great Britain"*. 'Coal came from Swanzy and merchandises from Bristol'. Iron, oil, wine, pitch, tar and hemp all came to local wharfs. Tobacco for some reason came from Barnstaple. Of course these were not available locally in a village which was otherwise near to being self-sufficient. The imports were mostly raw material for craftsmen, like iron for the blacksmith. Tobacco and illegal brandy would go direct to the innkeepers. There was no need yet for a shop. In return exports consisted of 'Fat oxen, as large and good as any in England, large Cheddar cheese, the greatest in England, and colts in great numbers'. The fields around the village were productive, so food was usually plentiful. The village bakery was in Mulberry Lane. Milk was available from dairies, and most other needs were met by local craftsmen. Itinerant tinkers might bring essential saucepans, and eye-catching hair ribbons, otherwise the village was indeed self-sufficient. Later, as fewer people grew their own food, and more worked elsewhere than on the land, general stores opened and deliveries were made of bread, milk, and meat.

In 1841 John Sellick of Hillside Farmhouse described himself as a grocer, by 1851 he became a 'shopkeeper'. He and his father provided gun powder for use in the quarry. Workers were paid a shilling a day, but powder cost £4 14s.11d. a month. His 'shop' however was merely a hatch into the hallway, or even an open window in the summer. A postcard of about 1900 shows a shop in Bridge Road run by G. Hawtin, eventually ending its days as an antique shop. At the end of the road, at Bridge Stores Mrs.Vinson sold ironmongery, boots, and cups and saucers, while her husband ran the garage. There were two other garages in the village. Central Garage, behind Church Cottages, where the bases of the petrol pumps still can be seen, built into the wall opposite the bus stop, and at Purn, the Fork Filling Station was run by Ray Goodall, who repaired cars, while Mr. Scotchmer sold the petrol, and charged accumulators for the early wireless sets.

When Hillcote was developed by 'Pussy' Perkins in the 1920s and 30s a shop opened there to serve the relatively isolated community at the top of the hill. At about the same time, Newbay Stores, a tobacconist and general store, opened near to the Queen's Hotel, as it was then called. For a short while 'Ye Olde Welle Shoppe' opened to sell what now might be called 'collectables', in part of the Well House. Incidentally, the form 'Ye' is incorrect. The Y involved is in fact a misuse of the Old English and Old Norse letter called 'Thorn'. It looked a bit like a Y, but was in fact a 'th' sound, so we should never say 'yee', and as for the extra e's on the ends! Well! It may have brought more customers, especially as it was painted with a 'Gothic' type face.

Beyond Bleadon Bridge, a roadside stall selling produce grown nearby, slowly developed over the years into Sanders' Supermarket. It achieved a high national reputation, providing a range and quality which was greatly missed by many villagers and visitors when it was 'disappeared', and became a site for houses. In the centre of the village the popular Post Office had started its days as a Receiving Office in 1833, where villagers could pay to collect whatever mail they might have. The Post Office eventually grew to become a well-stocked and well used conventional village shop, and as the others all closed one by one, it was the last to remain. When it finally went, the village was very fortunate that a Post Office was re-opened together with the latest reincarnation of the shop - a Country Store.

THE ROAD SOUTH
FROM WESTON WAS BUILT

Tnearly eighty years after the railway made the first cut through Bleadon Hill. The early 19th century population of Weston was no more than that of Bleadon. Without even a road to Uphill, the beach sufficed. The railway brought growth and prosperity from 1841. It also brought the need to deliver people to the stations from outlying areas. Later, with the advent of motor transport, the road network had to be considerably improved to increase access and reduce congestion. The original road south from Uphill crossed over the railway at Devil's Bridge, past Hillcote, or 'Pussytown', so called after its builder, 'Pussy' Perkins. It then followed the present road down through the village. Petrol for early motorists was available in the village at Central Garage, opposite the Rectory, and at Bridge Stores. Over the bridge, the early road meandered to left and right, to the Crescent, Hobb's Boat, Boat Lane, and Eastertown. An alternative at Uphill was to use the Turnpike level crossing, owned by the General Estates company, which avoided using the hill. This tollgate closed in 1908, having made £500 in its final year of operation. At a cost of £3000 the road then became the property of Weston Council. The maintenance of the six miles of road within the parish boundary of Bleadon was no longer the responsibility of the village after 1894.

In building the A370, the 'cutting' was excavated, and a bridge built over the railway. It had also caused the demolition of several cottages opposite the Anchor Inn. The new road cut through the centre of the little hamlet, burying its well, and forming another lay-by, Facum, or Fakenham Lane. In widening the road at that point, layers of natural gravel were cleared revealing the 'find' of reindeer antlers, referred to earlier. Local tenants had been allowed to use this filling for farm gateways, sand, shingle, fossils, and seashells. This sediment had been formed millions of years ago when Mendip was desert, surrounded by sea.

The bridge carrying the new road survived for about seventy years with few alterations until 2001, when it became necessary to make major repairs. The *Daily Telegraph* then describes how residents of Bleadon were given 'Passports' to enter the village, while the A370 was closed for the repairs to take place. Barriers were manned by Gurkhas who, contrary to some versions of the story, were not armed, neither was barbed wire in evidence! However according to the Temporary Traffic Regulation Order, it was an offence to use Bleadon as an alternative to crowded roads. For a short time the road through the village was very quiet.

Few people travelling past the Somerset levels on trunk roads or motorway will realise that they are passing the place where, four and a half thousand years ago, 'Sweet track man' had created his first 'road' across the marshes, just above water level. It could be said that this was the very beginning of road building in this country.

N THE NIGHT
OF 4th JANUARY
1941 WESTON SUPER MARE

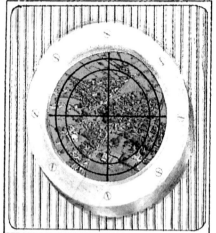

suffered its first major air raid of the second World War, from the German Luftwaffe. There were several targets: two aircraft factories, the Airport and Locking camp, where pilots were trained. Barrage balloons encircled the main targets, anti-aircraft guns with searchlights scanned the sky with 500 million candle power. However the most recent and secret form of defence were "Starfish" Q sites. Twelve encircled Bristol.

In Bleadon this took the form of a dummy airfield replicating the one in Weston. The aim was to distract the enemy planes to drop their bombs away from the real targets to an area where they would do little or no harm, in this case the Bleadon levels, near to the present treatment plant. The technique employed by the bombers was first to start fires with incendiary bombs, to identify the targets for the main force of planes, with their high explosive weapons. To provide a convincing imitation of the airport, false buildings were erected of wood and painted canvas, skilled work for redeployed film-set designers. The illusion was strengthened by having troughs of flammable material to simulate the incendiary bombs aimed to act as markers. These were electrically lit from the safety of the shelter housing the airmen controlling of the site.

On this night in 1941 much damage had been done in Weston, 34 people had been killed, 85 injured and many premises completely destroyed. The decision to activate the site at Bleadon was taken, but there was a major problem. Heavy rain that afternoon had affected the detonators. If the 'incendiaries' could not be lit, the planes would not be drawn away. Aircraftsman Cecil Bright though not in charge could see the problem, and the solution. He took petrol and worked his way 600 yards to the 'hangar' and lit the first fire. It took effect immediately bringing bombs all around. It was nearly two hours before he had finished lighting all the decoy fires and returned to the safety of the shelter.

For this courageous act Cecil Bright was awarded the Military Medal by the King. After the raid the next day 42 large craters and 1500 incendiary bombs were found. The only casualties had been some of Farmer Amesbury's dairy herd but how much worse might it not have been but for the actions of this brave man.

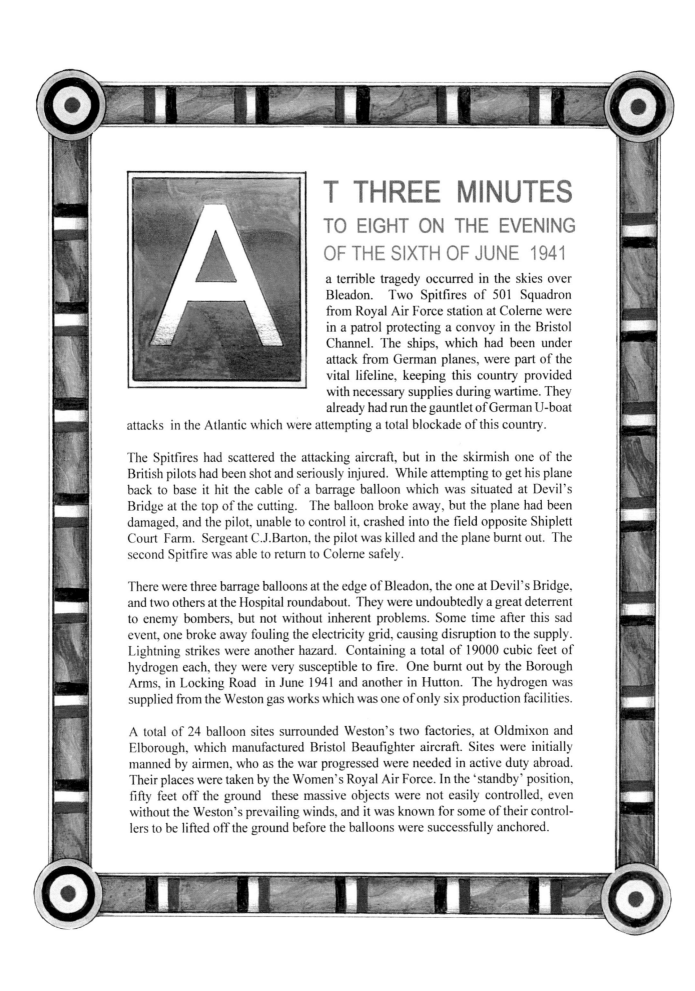

T THREE MINUTES
TO EIGHT ON THE EVENING
OF THE SIXTH OF JUNE 1941

a terrible tragedy occurred in the skies over Bleadon. Two Spitfires of 501 Squadron from Royal Air Force station at Colerne were in a patrol protecting a convoy in the Bristol Channel. The ships, which had been under attack from German planes, were part of the vital lifeline, keeping this country provided with necessary supplies during wartime. They already had run the gauntlet of German U-boat attacks in the Atlantic which were attempting a total blockade of this country.

The Spitfires had scattered the attacking aircraft, but in the skirmish one of the British pilots had been shot and seriously injured. While attempting to get his plane back to base it hit the cable of a barrage balloon which was situated at Devil's Bridge at the top of the cutting. The balloon broke away, but the plane had been damaged, and the pilot, unable to control it, crashed into the field opposite Shiplett Court Farm. Sergeant C.J.Barton, the pilot was killed and the plane burnt out. The second Spitfire was able to return to Colerne safely.

There were three barrage balloons at the edge of Bleadon, the one at Devil's Bridge, and two others at the Hospital roundabout. They were undoubtedly a great deterrent to enemy bombers, but not without inherent problems. Some time after this sad event, one broke away fouling the electricity grid, causing disruption to the supply. Lightning strikes were another hazard. Containing a total of 19000 cubic feet of hydrogen each, they were very susceptible to fire. One burnt out by the Borough Arms, in Locking Road in June 1941 and another in Hutton. The hydrogen was supplied from the Weston gas works which was one of only six production facilities.

A total of 24 balloon sites surrounded Weston's two factories, at Oldmixon and Elborough, which manufactured Bristol Beaufighter aircraft. Sites were initially manned by airmen, who as the war progressed were needed in active duty abroad. Their places were taken by the Women's Royal Air Force. In the 'standby' position, fifty feet off the ground these massive objects were not easily controlled, even without the Weston's prevailing winds, and it was known for some of their controllers to be lifted off the ground before the balloons were successfully anchored.

EONARD CAYGILL

was an engineer and inventor. His gravestone is in the churchyard in Bleadon. He was awarded the O.B.E. for his work on aircraft research and development. During World War II, he was part of the Dambusters team who built the bouncing bomb. Barnes Wallis had designed the weapon in 1939, but it was not produced until 1943. Caygill was involved with adapting the Lancaster bombers to carry and deliver the 9000 lb bombs. Originally spherical, but later cylindrical, the bombs were dropped at 30 feet, spinning, in order to bounce correctly.

After the war he worked on the Bristol Brabazon, which, unlike the elegant Concorde, never flew over Bleadon. It flew for 25 minutes over Avonmouth in 1949, but never received an airworthiness certificate. A cinema for 37 people, sleeping berths for 80, and dining room for 100, provided luxury travel, or would have done. The runway at Filton had to be extended from 2000 feet to 8000, causing the removal of the village of Charlton, and its inhabitants in a manner similar to that of the wealthy clients of Capability Brown in the 18th century.

The de Havilland Comet crashes of 1953, in Calcutta, Elba and Rome involved Caygill in a search for the cause of these disasters. He and his colleagues eventually discovered the 'unmistakable fingerprint of fatigue'. During the tests the fuselage was submerged many times, until the airframe fatigue was found, due to the shape of the windows causing a loss of air pressure.

When a later version of the Comet carried 80 Trans-Atlantic passengers in 1958, it was followed a few weeks later by a Boeing 707 carrying 120. Losing six years development time had probably led to the loss of the lead in the competitive North Atlantic routes, only re-established in 1999 with the European Airbus.

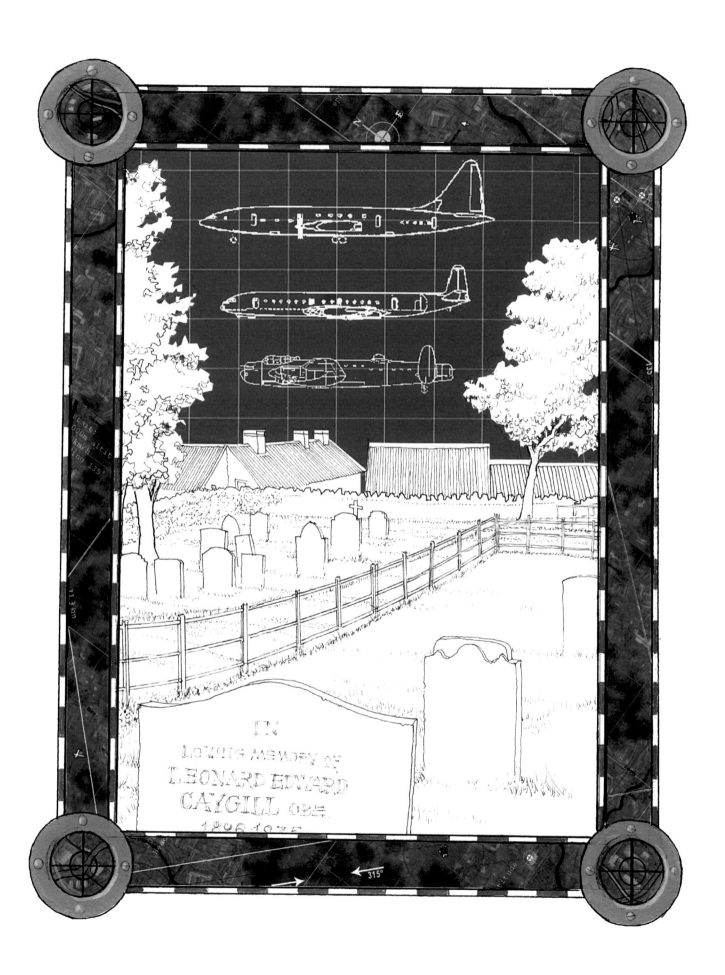

N A STRETCH OF THE
RIVER AXE UPSTREAM FROM

Bleadon Bridge, near Cow Bridge lay a favourite spot for swimming. A party of pupils from St. Christopher's, a Bristol school for the handicapped, was staying in Bleadon for the weekend. They were studying Esperanto under the guidance of Bert Over of The Mount and Edwin Clogg, who lived in a hut in the grounds of the house and who looked after the children in other huts. On Sunday 7th July 1957 the children went with Edwin for a swim in the river. The day had become cloudy and overcast so few anglers and walkers were around. David Ransley, a 15-year old, got into difficulties. Edwin dived in to help, but both disappeared under the water. Another pupil, a Swiss girl, dived in repeatedly to try to rescue them, but to no avail. They were both drowned. Police and ambulance were called, and the river was dragged for six hours. The following day, after a further two hours searching, their bodies were found in sixteen feet of water.

Edwin Hosken Clogg was well known to local children who spent much of their spare time in the grounds of The Mount. It was almost opposite the school in Shiplate Road. He and Bert Over, the owner, worked the market garden and orchards, always welcoming the help of the children, and frequently giving away more food than they kept. Other children visited, sometimes from a camp for under-privileged children near Winscombe, from which they were transported in style in a large 1928 Studebaker. This belonged to Bert's sister and was cared for and driven by Roy Goodall of the Fork Garage. It would have been capable of carrying any number of children before the days of seat belts and booster seats.

A tribute from the *Mercury* at the time tells how "few of the poorer folk of the district have not at some time had reason to be grateful to Edwin who was always seeking to help any who were finding life difficult, particularly if children were involved. Many too in hospitals and homes over a wide district were grateful for the gifts of fruit that arrived every summer." Edwin had been a successful business man earlier in his life, but "appalled by the greed and bitterness that marked our competitive system, he threw over all his gains to lead a simple life as a gardener, giving away most of what he grew to those in need. In his little hut in the grounds of The Mount his life might seem to have been austere, but no man could have been happier. In nature, particularly in birds, he found a never-failing interest, and there was no finer authority on the birds of the district."

Although he was 71 at the time of this tragedy, Edwin's energy was remarkable. He was known to have walked 40 miles across Exmoor in poor weather, had a simple meal at a Youth Hostel, taken a stroll and then played six games of table tennis, at which he excelled. His principles had led him to be a conscientious objector, which demanded a particular form of courage during wartime, and he died attempting something that typified his life and character, trying to help a child in trouble. On his gravestone in the churchyard, subscribed for by villagers, is written 'A life given for another'.
The initial is adapted from a commercial design of the 1950s. The word Courage has a totally different connotation, but its use nevertheless seemed appropriate when applied to the life of Edwin Clogg.

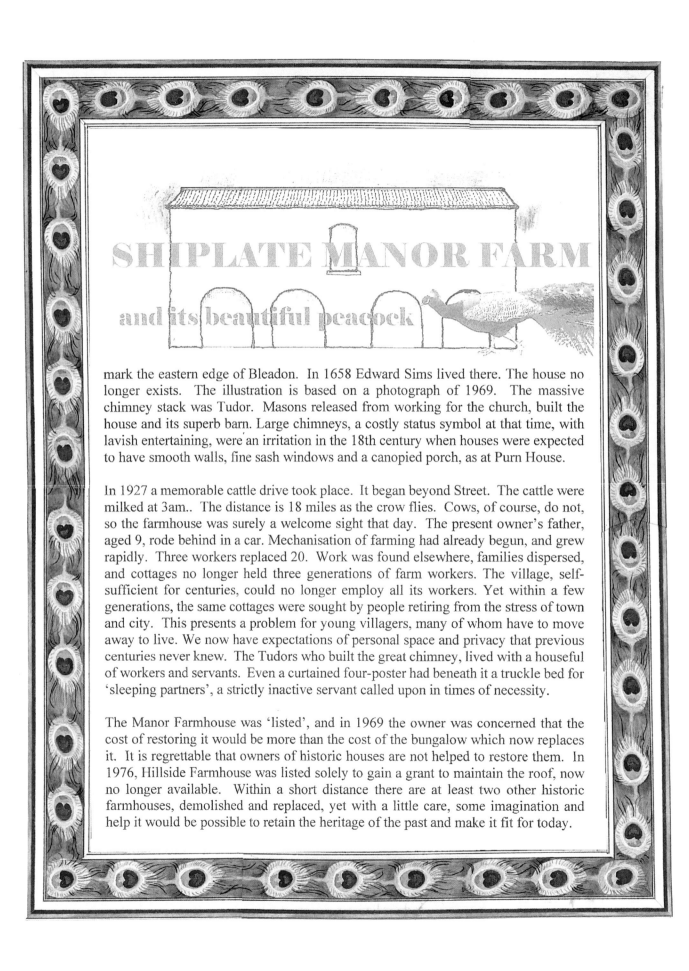

SHIPLATE MANOR FARM

and its beautiful peacock

mark the eastern edge of Bleadon. In 1658 Edward Sims lived there. The house no longer exists. The illustration is based on a photograph of 1969. The massive chimney stack was Tudor. Masons released from working for the church, built the house and its superb barn. Large chimneys, a costly status symbol at that time, with lavish entertaining, were an irritation in the 18th century when houses were expected to have smooth walls, fine sash windows and a canopied porch, as at Purn House.

In 1927 a memorable cattle drive took place. It began beyond Street. The cattle were milked at 3am.. The distance is 18 miles as the crow flies. Cows, of course, do not, so the farmhouse was surely a welcome sight that day. The present owner's father, aged 9, rode behind in a car. Mechanisation of farming had already begun, and grew rapidly. Three workers replaced 20. Work was found elsewhere, families dispersed, and cottages no longer held three generations of farm workers. The village, self-sufficient for centuries, could no longer employ all its workers. Yet within a few generations, the same cottages were sought by people retiring from the stress of town and city. This presents a problem for young villagers, many of whom have to move away to live. We now have expectations of personal space and privacy that previous centuries never knew. The Tudors who built the great chimney, lived with a houseful of workers and servants. Even a curtained four-poster had beneath it a truckle bed for 'sleeping partners', a strictly inactive servant called upon in times of necessity.

The Manor Farmhouse was 'listed', and in 1969 the owner was concerned that the cost of restoring it would be more than the cost of the bungalow which now replaces it. It is regrettable that owners of historic houses are not helped to restore them. In 1976, Hillside Farmhouse was listed solely to gain a grant to maintain the roof, now no longer available. Within a short distance there are at least two other historic farmhouses, demolished and replaced, yet with a little care, some imagination and help it would be possible to retain the heritage of the past and make it fit for today.

EVERE WEATHER IS RECORDED AS EARLY AS

the year 1185. Quite specifically it is announced that 'on the Monday before Easter, chanced a sore earthquake throughout all parts of the land, such as had not been heard of in England since the beginning of the world'. Our version, lacking the drama, might read 'since records began'. Stone houses were 'overthrown, and the great church at Lincoln was rent from the top downwards'. There had been an even earlier earthquake recorded in Somerset and Gloucester on 25th July, 1122, and Wells Cathedral had been badly damaged by another in 1248. Two cathedrals being hit might seem surprising, but these were the only really large buildings at the time. Wells had only been started in 1180, and consecrated in 1239. Battlements, capitals and columns fell, but it is difficult to trace if there had been any structural damage to be repaired. Another earthquake destroyed St. Michael's church on the Tor, in Glastonbury on 11th September 1275, which also caused damage to the Abbey.

Possibly the coldest day ever in this country, was during the two months of frost in 1664-65. Many sheep died ten years later as a result of 13 days of continuous snow in March. In winter of 1683-84, the ground in Somerset froze to a depth of four feet. In *Lorna Doone* by R.D.Blackmore, he describes how 'strong men broke three pickaxes' and 'scarcely 1 in 10 of the sheep and cattle were saved,' during that winter. Snowdrifts on Christmas Day 1836 completely blocked roads, with even bigger drifts in 1849. Fifteen feet of drifts in the winter of 1880-81, led to 200 labourers being employed to clear the way from Uphill to Rooksbridge.

Mists and fog also have proved to be hazardous. In 1898, Ann and Charles Banwell, a couple from Bleadon were walking home after an evening at the *Anchor*. He arrived home first, and went to bed, but poor Ann never reached home, she had fallen into a rhyne, and drowned. Children, too, have fallen victim while playing on the ice of the frozen River Axe.

Sunday, December the 13th 1981, was the day when the sea defences at Uphill were breached. Snow in the morning, became heavier, 10cms. by lunchtime turning to torrential rain, an inch by the evening. Widespread flooding ensued, causing great damage, which led to a much improved flood defence system. October 15th, 1987 was the day of the hurricane which was not forecast, but which nevertheless came. It uprooted many thousands of trees, although this part of the country suffered less than some. Later, in July 1991, heavy rain nearly washed away the efforts of the workers creating 'Jill's Garden', in Grove Park, Weston. Two inches were recorded overnight, whereas the yearly average for rain in Bleadon is 35 inches. When the weathercock on Bleadon church was damaged by storm in 1933, it was too costly to restore, but fortunately for weather watchers, it was regilded and refitted in 1995, a few years after the trees in the vicarage garden had been uprooted, opposite.

BLEADON SUMMER MAY DAY CELEBRATIONS

Earliest celebrations of May Day were Anglo-Saxon, or even Iron Age in origin. By 1350 all of southern England celebrated the end of seed sowing and the start of Spring, a rare holiday for farm workers. It has not been continuous. Objections to its pagan origin caused a ban in Bristol in 1549, and Puritans cut maypoles in half to make ladders.. The Restoration saw a 130 ft. high maypole in the Strand, taller than a nearby steeple. Robert Herrick wrote "There's not a budding boy or girl this day, but is got up and gone to bring in May." May Day was perhaps too rustic for the eighteenth century, and too frivolous for the nineteenth. The twentieth saw old traditions recreated and better appreciated

Originally there were three elements to the festivities, maypoles, Morris men and May Queens. It is believed Bleadon's school had a maypole and enough children to dance around it, but it is not certain they ever did. Maypoles were often a source of great inter-village rivalry, and even theft. There was another use to which they were put. Men of the village measured their feet against the pole, and used it to mark out the site for a new building. A cottage would be 12 feet by 24, and a farmhouse 16 feet by 32.

Morris men have a 500 year old tradition in England. In Henry VII's time they were so called because of a perceived likeness to Moorish dancing. In some Morris traditions 'Sweeps' dress in black rags and tatters and colour their faces, adding to this perception. Bleadon's regular visitors,the Chalice Morris men have kept the tradition thriving for forty years, dressed in white, the Cotswold form, with red baldrics, (so *that* is where the name comes from) a Chalice symbol at their backs and their personal symbol in front.

As for the May Queen, it was said of her if she washed her face in morning dew on May Day she would be even more beautiful, but sadly Bleadon no longer seeks to crown her.

May Day holiday became official in 1978 and Bleadon's celebrations became linked to that day. It had its origins long ago with Church Fetes on the Rectory lawn at a time when public expectations were less demanding. Attempts to keep up with today's constantly changing expectations are successful, as can be seen by the numbers of visitors to Bleadon May Day Fair, but it is still dependent on the voluntary efforts of villagers who seek to continue the tradition of a community celebrating together. It is increasingly difficult to provide something different or memorable, at a time when celebrating is a relatively commonplace occupation.

CIDER ORCHARDS

large and small have been part of this landscape for centuries. In the Iron Age, Bleadon man ate apples and made a primitive cider. The Romans had over 20 varieties of apples, but it was in Mediaeval times that the cultivation of orchards became organised, by the monasteries. Among the earliest varieties, Pearmains were valuable enough to be part of a payment to the Crown in 1205. They and Costard cooking apples were the most popular, the latter being sold in London by the original 'Costardmongers' at fourpence a hundred in the fifteenth century.

Most orchards in Bleadon were on the slopes behind Purn Way and in Shiplate, with smaller ones dotted around the village. There was a cider press at Manor Farm, and probably others in the village. In early days, travelling presses were carried on wagons and trailers to wherever they were needed.

The '*Victoria*' was a cider and beer house in Bridge Road, where jugs being taken home to the 'master' were often diluted at the village pump. This was probably a nineteenth century establishment, or perhaps renamed from earlier days. The last landladies were the Misses Payne, one of whom was a hearty drinker, and donated some of her profits to carpeting the church. Among their last customers in the 1940s would have been soldiers based at an anti-aircraft gun post on Bleadon Hill, near Hillcote.

A more notorious place, *'The Old Ferry House'* stood near Hobbs Boat Inn. It was known as a 'German House', in the tradition of ascribing unwanted phenomena to other nations, like measles, 'flu', and Elm disease, . There bread and cheese was one penny, and cider or beer was free. For many years this had caused problems to the village, either as a rival to their local, or due to rowdiness. In 1840 when the 'navigators' were working on the railway line and probably grateful for cheap food and free beer, things became intolerable and the villagers summoned official help. The owner brandished a gun, and his wife a pickaxe, but the villagers overcame them and demolished the place.

The origins of many pubs came from the early 16th century, when a building near the church was used for making ale or cider. The Church House became the pub, in which bowls and skittles were played, and itinerant musicians entertained. These traditions are well kept today, and after entertaining the villagers, Morris Men and visiting choirs take refreshment at the *Queen's,* as in earlier days, when it was of course the *King's Arms.*

The future of cider orchards in Bleadon could hardly be in better shape now that many thousands of new trees have been planted in Shiplate. They will soon be contributing to maintain the reputation and historical traditions of Somerset cider.

For the first time in many centuries perhaps for the first time since it was settled, there is no dairy herd within the village of Bleadon. The milk we drink, and the cheese we eat now comes from elsewhere. Globalisation has become one of many factors affecting farming today. Another, as always, is the weather, now seemingly less temperate, with the three warmest years on record within the last ten, and the coldest January, and wettest April, paradoxically declared within a period of drought.

With this in mind the farmer now has to grow crops that are more hardy, and yet must be in demand, requiring foresight, imagination, and considerable understanding of the global scheme of things. Prices of such crops can vary wildly, often rendering the developing countries most vulnerable.

Globalisation has led, by definition, to an increased use of transport and consequent pollution, a third factor. Historically this is no new phenomenon. Previous generations were familiar with horse-drawn farm machinery, as we see opposite. Horse power had always provided the main means of transport in the countryside and in towns and cities. They were fed on oats from the farm, but a great deal of pollution was caused in cities.

Yet another factor for the farmer's consideration are today's technological innovations . These have led to wheat being grown to be converted into petrol, and oilseed being converted into diesel. Satellite imagery, such as part of the map of Bleadon shown in the initial above, is another example of the advances in technology being harnessed for use on today's farms.

From being almost self-sufficient a few centuries ago, Bleadon now is being drawn inexorably into the "global village" The age-old problem for the farmer remains, however, and it is highly significant that the world's largest computers are now being set the task of more accurately forecasting the weather.

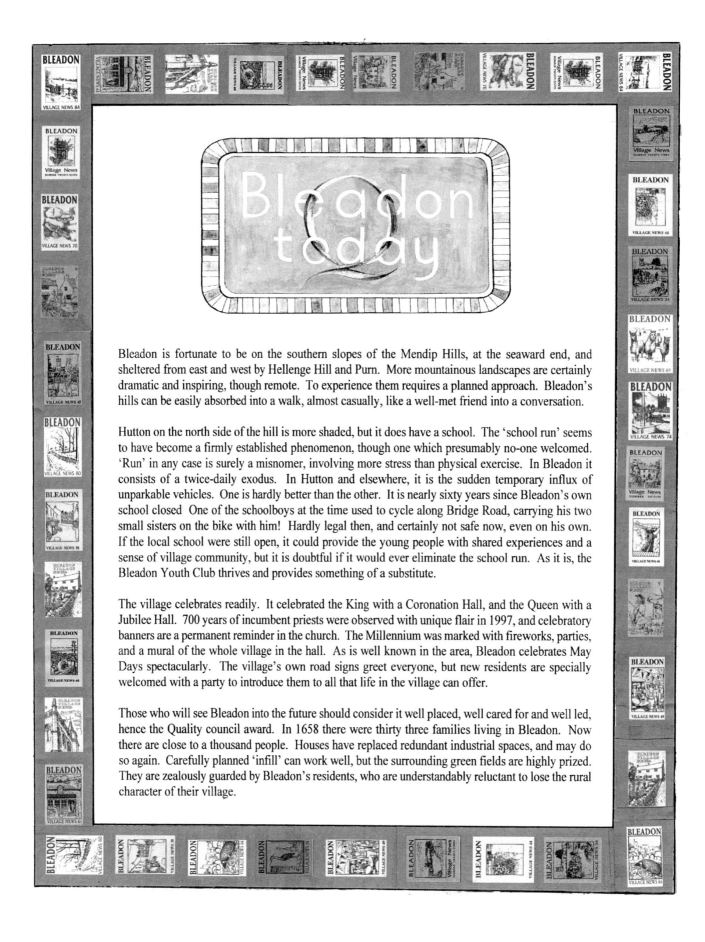

Bleadon today

Bleadon is fortunate to be on the southern slopes of the Mendip Hills, at the seaward end, and sheltered from east and west by Hellenge Hill and Purn. More mountainous landscapes are certainly dramatic and inspiring, though remote. To experience them requires a planned approach. Bleadon's hills can be easily absorbed into a walk, almost casually, like a well-met friend into a conversation.

Hutton on the north side of the hill is more shaded, but it does have a school. The 'school run' seems to have become a firmly established phenomenon, though one which presumably no-one welcomed. 'Run' in any case is surely a misnomer, involving more stress than physical exercise. In Bleadon it consists of a twice-daily exodus. In Hutton and elsewhere, it is the sudden temporary influx of unparkable vehicles. One is hardly better than the other. It is nearly sixty years since Bleadon's own school closed One of the schoolboys at the time used to cycle along Bridge Road, carrying his two small sisters on the bike with him! Hardly legal then, and certainly not safe now, even on his own. If the local school were still open, it could provide the young people with shared experiences and a sense of village community, but it is doubtful if it would ever eliminate the school run. As it is, the Bleadon Youth Club thrives and provides something of a substitute.

The village celebrates readily. It celebrated the King with a Coronation Hall, and the Queen with a Jubilee Hall. 700 years of incumbent priests were observed with unique flair in 1997, and celebratory banners are a permanent reminder in the church. The Millennium was marked with fireworks, parties, and a mural of the whole village in the hall. As is well known in the area, Bleadon celebrates May Days spectacularly. The village's own road signs greet everyone, but new residents are specially welcomed with a party to introduce them to all that life in the village can offer.

Those who will see Bleadon into the future should consider it well placed, well cared for and well led, hence the Quality council award. In 1658 there were thirty three families living in Bleadon. Now there are close to a thousand people. Houses have replaced redundant industrial spaces, and may do so again. Carefully planned 'infill' can work well, but the surrounding green fields are highly prized. They are zealously guarded by Bleadon's residents, who are understandably reluctant to lose the rural character of their village.

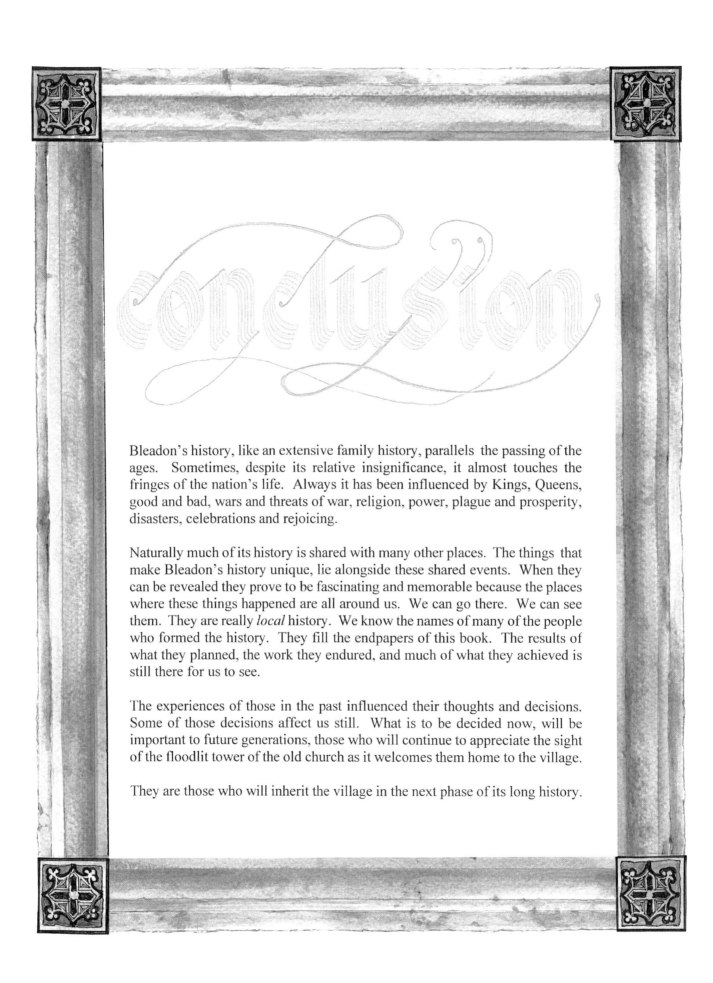

Conclusion

Bleadon's history, like an extensive family history, parallels the passing of the ages. Sometimes, despite its relative insignificance, it almost touches the fringes of the nation's life. Always it has been influenced by Kings, Queens, good and bad, wars and threats of war, religion, power, plague and prosperity, disasters, celebrations and rejoicing.

Naturally much of its history is shared with many other places. The things that make Bleadon's history unique, lie alongside these shared events. When they can be revealed they prove to be fascinating and memorable because the places where these things happened are all around us. We can go there. We can see them. They are really *local* history. We know the names of many of the people who formed the history. They fill the endpapers of this book. The results of what they planned, the work they endured, and much of what they achieved is still there for us to see.

The experiences of those in the past influenced their thoughts and decisions. Some of those decisions affect us still. What is to be decided now, will be important to future generations, those who will continue to appreciate the sight of the floodlit tower of the old church as it welcomes them home to the village.

They are those who will inherit the village in the next phase of its long history.

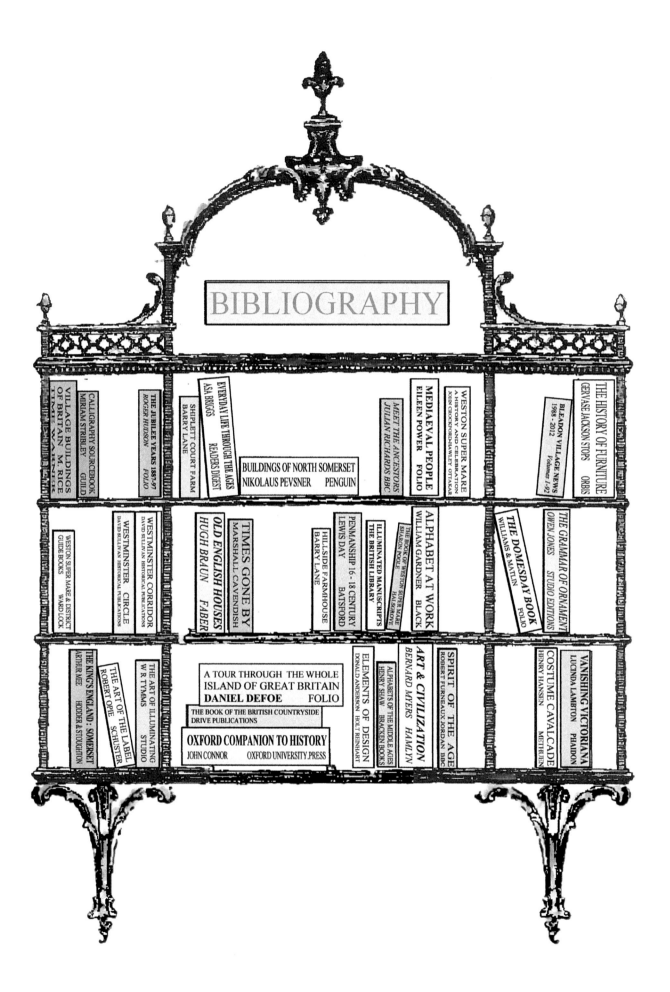

BIBLIOGRAPHY

VILLAGE BUILDINGS OF BRITAIN M. RICE TIME WARNER

CALLIGRAPHY SOURCEBOOK MIRIAM STRIBLEY GUILD

THE JUBILEE YEARS 1887-97 ROGER HUDSON FOLIO

SHIPLETT COURT FARM BARRY LANE

EVERYDAY LIFE THROUGH THE AGES ASA BRIGGS READERS DIGEST

BUILDINGS OF NORTH SOMERSET NIKOLAUS PEVSNER PENGUIN

MEET THE ANCESTORS JULIAN RICHARDS BBC

MEDIAEVAL PEOPLE EILEEN POWER FOLIO

WESTON SUPER MARE A HISTORY AND CELEBRATION JOHN CROCKFORD-HAWLEY OTTAKAR

BLEADON VILLAGE NEWS 1988 - 2012 Volumes 1-92

THE HISTORY OF FURNITURE GERVASE JACKSON STOPS ORBIS

WESTON SUPER MARE & DISTRICT GUIDE BOOKS WARD LOCK

WESTMINSTER CIRCLE DAVID SULLIVAN HISTORICAL PUBLICATIONS

WESTMINSTER CORRIDOR DAVID SULLIVAN HISTORICAL PUBLICATIONS

OLD ENGLISH HOUSES HUGH BRAUN FABER

TIMES GONE BY MARSHALL CAVENDISH

HILLSIDE FARMHOUSE BARRY LANE

PENMANSHIP 16 - 18 CENTURY LEWIS DAY BATSFORD

ILLUMINATED MANUSCRIPTS THE BRITISH LIBRARY

THE BOOK OF WESTON SUPER MARE SHARON POOLE HALSGROVE

ALPHABET AT WORK WILLIAM GARDNER BLACK

THE DOMESDAY BOOK WILLIAMS & MATLIN FOLIO

THE GRAMMAR OF ORNAMENT OWEN JONES STUDIO EDITIONS

THE KING'S ENGLAND: SOMERSET ARTHUR MEE HODDER & STOUGHTON

THE ART OF THE LABEL ROBERT OPIE SCHUSTER

THE ART OF ILLUMINATING W R TYMMS STUDIO

A TOUR THROUGH THE WHOLE ISLAND OF GREAT BRITAIN DANIEL DEFOE FOLIO

THE BOOK OF THE BRITISH COUNTRYSIDE DRIVE PUBLICATIONS

OXFORD COMPANION TO HISTORY JOHN CONNOR OXFORD UNIVERSITY PRESS

ELEMENTS OF DESIGN DONALD ANDERSON HOLT REINHART

ALPHABETS OF THE MIDDLE AGES HENRY SHAW BRACKEN BOOKS

ART & CIVILIZATION BERNARD MYERS HAMLYN

SPIRIT OF THE AGE ROBERT FURNEAUX JORDAN BBC

COSTUME CAVALCADE HENRY HANSEN METHUEN

VANISHING VICTORIANA LUCINDA LAMBTON PHAIDON

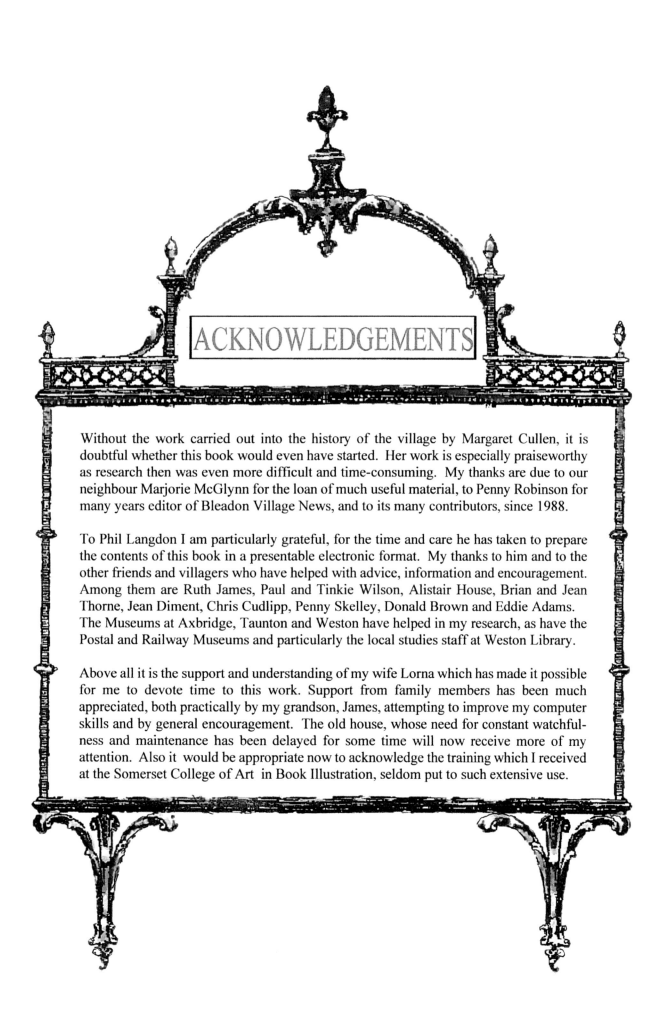

ACKNOWLEDGEMENTS

Without the work carried out into the history of the village by Margaret Cullen, it is doubtful whether this book would even have started. Her work is especially praiseworthy as research then was even more difficult and time-consuming. My thanks are due to our neighbour Marjorie McGlynn for the loan of much useful material, to Penny Robinson for many years editor of Bleadon Village News, and to its many contributors, since 1988.

To Phil Langdon I am particularly grateful, for the time and care he has taken to prepare the contents of this book in a presentable electronic format. My thanks to him and to the other friends and villagers who have helped with advice, information and encouragement. Among them are Ruth James, Paul and Tinkie Wilson, Alistair House, Brian and Jean Thorne, Jean Diment, Chris Cudlipp, Penny Skelley, Donald Brown and Eddie Adams. The Museums at Axbridge, Taunton and Weston have helped in my research, as have the Postal and Railway Museums and particularly the local studies staff at Weston Library.

Above all it is the support and understanding of my wife Lorna which has made it possible for me to devote time to this work. Support from family members has been much appreciated, both practically by my grandson, James, attempting to improve my computer skills and by general encouragement. The old house, whose need for constant watchfulness and maintenance has been delayed for some time will now receive more of my attention. Also it would be appropriate now to acknowledge the training which I received at the Somerset College of Art in Book Illustration, seldom put to such extensive use.

Richard Pay 1297 John de Astewlby 1311 Alewy de la Leo 1327 Simon de Brstol 1327

John Gadd George Edwards George Taylor William Bird Thomas Durstor

Robert Bayley James Bayley William Bayley Thomas Haynes John Pipe

William Seaman Samuel Palmer Mrs Nancy Bayley David Crandon Mr. Dear

Jessy Dyer William Tripp Abraham Slade John Crandon Robert Amesbury

Thomas Evans George Harden Goerge Cottle Harry Cook Joseph Cottl

James Corfield William Lusher John Riden Samuel Lacy Dorothy Lacy

Thomas Bokenhulle 1348 Thomas Raly 1348 William Excestre 1406 Robert Thurburt

William Keate Jacob Carpenter James Sellick John Sellick Mary Sellick

Abraham Slade Charles Bailey Harry Crandon Chapman Langford John Champion

George Edwards Sarah Andrews Jane Sellick Mary Sellick Hannah Adam

Thomas Wickham Matthew Woodford Edward Rattue David Moncrieff John Price

Selena Boley Thomas Jones William Jones Mary Jones John Jones

William Whyting 1433 Nicholas Easton 1436 William More 1440 William Gifford 1469

Charles Chidwell James Barton William Cordwell Thomas Keast Mary Keast

John Clark Martha Clark Edward Crandon Mary Crandon Emily Crandor

Charles Bailey Sarah Bailey Hannah Thomas William Taylor Elizabeth Taylo

Abraham Jeans Henry Taylor Hester Jeans Robert Grinter Elizabeth Grinter

William Wryxham 1470 John Perche 1472 Stephen Tyler 147 Nicholas Cleve 1487

Mary Parker John Watts Louisa Watts Mary Lovell George Podge

Charles Shriven Sarah Shriven George Edwards Tamar Edwards Mary Edwards

Mary Amesbury Charles Edwards Louisa Grinter William Grinter John Cuff

George Tanner Emma Tanner John Thresher George Parsons Lydia Parsons

Mary Phillips Martha Llewellin Annie Llewellin Anne Gould Hannah Gould

Edward Powell 1501 John Ball 1540 John Sprint 1581 William Austin 158

Frederick Boley Sarah Bailey Mary Dunscombe Harriet Burrows Alice Burrows

Jesse Coles Rose Coles Beatrice Coles George Drake Alice Parkhouse Olive Perry

Ellen Barber Arthur Stone Alice Stone John Stear Anne Stear Mary Scrivens

John Walmesley 1604 Thomas Macarnesse 1619 Meric Casaubon 1625 Thomas Taylor